PEDAGOGY OF ISLAM

About the Editor

Dr. Mujibul Hasan Siddiqui, M.A. (Economics), M.Ed., M.Phil. (Education), Ph.D. (Education), PGDHE, PGDDE, MADE, CCCA, CCPALA is working as Associate Professor in the Department of Education, Aligarh Muslim University, Aligarh-202002, Uttar Pradesh, India. He has also worked as Acting Chairperson of the Department of Education, Aligarh Muslim University, Aligarh. He has authored and edited several books, encyclopaedias in the area of education, research and innovative teaching, published more than fifty research papers, reviewed eighty national and international research papers. He has attended several national and international seminars, workshops, conferences in India. He is a member of Scientific Advisory Committee of International Conferences, USA IISTE Journal of Education and Practice, IISTE International Institute of Science Technology and Education, Accelerating Global Knowledge, Creation and Sharing IISTE USA P.O. Box 5934, New York, NY 10016 USA and Institute of Knowledge, Sri Lanka and India. He is a member of editorial board of several national and international journals of research. He has guided several Ph.D. research scholars and research projects of M.Ed. students in the area of curriculum, Planning, ICT, Models of Teaching, Higher Education, Management of Education, Educational Psychology, Philosophy etc. He has guided Research Projects of the students of Indira Gandhi National Open University, India. He is the foreign examiner of Ph.D. research scholars and M.Ed. Students and evaluated Ph.D. theses and Dissertations in faculty of education of the University of South Africa (UNISA) and University of Zululand, South Africa. He has received many academic and research excellence awards in India like Life Time Education Achievement Award, Bharat Gaurav Ratan Award, Best Educationist Award, Bharat Shiksha Ratan Award, Eminent Educationist Award, Rashtriya Vidya Saraswati Puraskar. He has visited Lootah Groups of Companies as Educational Advisor, Dubai, UAE. He is the life member of several research and educational organisations in India like All India Association of Muslim Social Scientists, India; All India Association of Educational Research, India; All India Federation of Educational Associations, India. All India Association of Teacher Educators, New Delhi, Member in the International Panel of the Board of Research Advisors North Corolina, U.S.A. Vice-President of Commonwealth Association for Educational Administration and Management, Uttar Pradesh. He is Editor-in-Chief and Publisher of Five International Journals: 1. Excellence International Journal of Education and Research ISSN 2322-0147 (Online Journal), 2. Excellence International Journal of Education and Research ISSN 2349-8838 (Print Journal), 3. Excellence International Journal of Scientific Research ISSN 2394-4242 (Print Journal), 4. Excellence International Journal of Islamic Studies and Theological Research ISSN 2394-6830 (Print Journal), and 5. Excellence International Journal of Psychological and Mental Health Research ISSN 2395-5643 (Print Journal).

PEDAGOGY OF ISLAM

Edited by
Mujibul Hasan Siddiqui

CONCEPT PUBLISHING COMPANY PVT. LTD.
NEW DELHI-110059

ISBN-13: 978-93-88937-57-3

First Published 2020

Published and Printed by

Concept Since 1974

Concept Publishing Company Pvt. Ltd.
A/15-16, Commercial Block, Mohan Garden,
New Delhi-110059 (INDIA)
T : 91 11 25351460, 91 11 25351794
E : publishing@conceptpub.com; *W* : www.conceptpub.com

Cataloging in Publication Data--Courtesy: D.K. Agencies (P) Ltd. <docinfo@dkagencies.com>

Pedagogy of Islam / edited by Mujibul Hasan Siddiqui.
pages cm
Contributed articles.
Includes bibliographical references and index.
ISBN 9789388937573

1. Islam—Study and teaching. 2. Islamic education. I. Siddiqui, Mujibul Hasan, editor.

LCC BP42.I85 2020 | DDC 297.071 23

Introduction /Preface

This book entitled "Pedagogy of Islam" consists of twelve chapters, penned by different scholars in their area of specialisation.

The chapter first focuses on conceptual and historical aspects of Islam.

The chapter second gives emphasis on aims and objectives of education in Islam.

The chapter third highlights meaning of life in context of Islam.

The chapter fourth describes history, aims and objectives of Islamic education and importance of education in Islam.

The chapter fifth states about conceptual, theoretical and research aspect of curriculum.

The chapter sixth explains the initiative taken to reform Islamic curriculum.

The chapter seventh describes the meaning of Islamic curriculum and its origin and other aspects like need and importance of curriculum, and types of curriculum.

The chapter eighth describes various innovative methods of teaching in Islamic studies.

The chapter ninth describes methods of education and teaching in Islam.

The chapter tenth highlights various types of teaching aids in Islamic studies.

The chapter eleventh describes various techniques of evaluation in teaching of Islam.

The chapter twelfth explains the lesson planning in teaching of Islam. This chapter also provides one sample of lesson plan in teaching of Islam.

Contents

List of Contributors

Anjum Ahmed, Assistant Professor, Department of Education, Aligarh Muslim University, Aligarh **Email Id:** *anjum.amu1312@gmail.com*

Aquib Akhtar, Junior Research Fellow, UGC Department of Education, Aligarh Muslim University, Aligarh.
Email Id: *aquibsikander@gmail.com*

Barkat Para, M.Phil. (Education) MANNU Hydcrabad, Research Scholar, Department of Education, Aligarh Muslim University, Aligarh.
Email Id: *bhusain114@gmail.com*

Brenny Novriansyah, Research Scholar, Department of Education, Aligarh Muslim University, Aligarh. **Email Id:** *brennynovriansyh@gmail.com*

Hussein Ahmed Abdo Rajhy. Email Id: *husseinrajhy@gmail.com*

Iemon Jan, Junior Research Fellow, Department of Islamic Studies, University of Kashmir. **Email Id:** *Miraiman2@gmail.com*

Kounsar Jabeen, Research Scholar, Department of Education, Aligarh Muslim University, Aligarh. **Email Id:** *kysarmohd001@gmail.com*

Madiha Parvez, Research Scholar, Department of Education, Aligarh Muslim University, Aligarh. **Email Id:** *madihaparvez3@gmail.com*

Mohd Zubair Kales, Associate Professor in Education, Govt. College of Education, Canal Road, Jammu. **Email Id:** *mzkales@gmail.com*

Mudassir, Research Scholar, Department of Education, Aligarh Muslim University, Aligarh, U.P. **Email Id:** *mudasirhamid77@gmail.com*

Nasrin, Department of Education, Aligarh Muslim University, Aligarh, U.P. **Email Id:** *nasrinamu@gmail.com*

Noor Aisha, M.Ed. (Ex-student) N.K.B.M.G. P.G. College, Chandausi M.J.P. Rohilkhand University, Bareilly. **Email Id:** *nor.aisha70@gmail.com*

Shaikh Haroon Moinuddin, Email: *shmiase@gmail.com*

Tariq Anwar, Badaun, U.P. **Email Id:** *drtariqueanwar1@gmail.com, drtariqueanwar@ yahoo.co.in*

1
Concept of Islam

Iemon Jan

Islam is a complete way of life. It aims at constructing the entire fabric of human life and culture on the firm foundation of ethical values and principles revealed by Almighty Allah for man's guidance. Islam is an Arabic word, which not only means submission (to God) but also means peace. It also means acceptance and commitment to abide by the teachings and guidance of Allah. One of the beautiful names of Allah is As-Salam (the peace). Islam also means to be at peace with Allah and His creatures. Being at peace with Allah implies complete submission to His will, Who is the source of all purity and goodness. Being at peace with His creatures implies living in peace within one's self, with other people and with the environment. Thus, Islam is a total system of living in peace. The name Islam is universal in meaning. Islam is not named after a tribe of people or an individual, as Judaism is named after the tribe of Judah, Christianity after Christ and Buddhism after Buddha. Islam is not a name chosen by human beings; it was divinely communicated from Allah. Islam is a global faith, not of the East or the West, Islam is a complete way of life, implying total submission to Allah. One who follows and surrenders his or her will to Allah, voluntarily, is called a Muslim (Arabic word which means, the one who submits to the will of Allah).[1] It was not Muhammad (saw) but Adam (as) who first brought Islam to humanity. Then, each Prophet and Messenger came to exhort the people to a clear understanding of God's commandments. They offered teachings relevant to that time, until Allah chose the final prophet, Muhammad (saw), to come with the last testament referred to as the Qur'an.

Say, "*we believe in Allah, and in what has been revealed to us and what was revealed to Abraham, Ismael, Isaac, Jacob and the tribes, and in (the books) given to Moses, Jesus and the prophets, from their Lord. We make no distinction between one and another among them, and to Allah do we bow our will (in-Islam).*"[2]

Allah is an Arabic word, meaning, 'The one and only True Deity', the proper name of The One who created the heavens and the earth. Arabic-speaking Jews and Christians also call God by the name Allah. For a Muslim, Allah is the greatest and the most inclusive of names for God, denoting The One who is adored in worship, The One who created all that exists.

Islam is the continuation and culmination of all the preceding revealed religions and hence it is for all times and all peoples. No other revealed religion has any convincing claim to provide guidance in all walks of human life for all times. But Islam addresses humanity at large and offers basic guidance regarding all human problems.

Islam has laid down universal fundamental rights for humanity as a whole, which are to be observed and respected under all circumstances. To achieve these rights Islam provides not only legal safeguards but also a very effective moral system. Thus, whatever leads to the welfare of the individual or the society is morally good in Islam and whatever is injurious is morally bad. Islam attaches so much importance to the love of God and love of man that it warns against too much of formalism.

We read in the Qur'an: "*it is not righteousness that ye turn your faces towards east or west; but it is righteousness— to believe in Allah and the last day and the Angels, and the book, and the Messengers; to spend of your substance, out of love for Him, for your kin, for orphans, for the needy, for the wayfarer, for those who ask. And for the ransom of slaves; to be steadfasting prayer and give Zakah, to fulfil the contracts which ye have made; and to be firm and patient, in pain and adversity, and throughout all periods of panic. Such are the people of truth, the God-fearing.*"[3]

The Concept of *Tauheed* (oneness of God)

The term is derived from the three Arab consonants root waw-ha-dal, which serves as the vehicle for the basic concept of '**oneness**' or '**unity**' along with the closely related ideas of '**singularity**' and

'uniqueness.' These root letters are clearly apparent in the numerical adjective Wahid (one) as stated in the Qur'an:

> "*Your God is surely one.*"[4]

The term Tauheed demands a lengthier translation, namely: "the realization and affirmation of oneness." The unity of God, the Divine unity, unity in its most profound sense. Allah is the Real, the Absolute. Allah is one in His essence, His Attributes and His Acts. The unity of Allah is a beautiful concept, and Muslims reaffirm their adherence to it many times a day, when they perform Salah and when they recite Shahada in tashahud, one of the requisite in performing Salah. To acknowledge the fact of the "affirmation-of-Oneness" renew your faith by frequent invocation of "*la ilaha illa llah*" (**there is none worthy of worship accept Allah)** will be the means to eradicate Shirk (polytheism).

The foundation of the Islamic faith is belief in the oneness of Almighty Allah, the God of Ibrahim, Nuh, Musa and Isa. Muslims believe in one, unique, incomparable God, Who has no son or partner, and that none has the right to be worshipped but Him alone. He is the rule God, and every other deity is false. He has the most magnificent names and sublime perfect attributes. No one shares His divinity, nor His attributes. In the Qur'an, God describes Himself:

> "*Say, He is God, the One. God, to Whom the creatures turn for their needs. He begets not, nor was He begotten, and there is none like Him.*"[5]

Sources of Islam

It has been a habit for adherents of abrogated religions and man-made creeds to hallow their inherited books, which were written since ancient times and whose authors or translators or the time of their writing may not really be known. They were just written by some people who used to suffer from what other human beings suffer from like weakness, defect and forgetfulness.

As for the Qur'an, it is different from all other books in that, it depends on the true source which is the divine revelation: the Qur'an and Sunnah.

The Glorious Qur'an

Islam is the religion of Allah that was why Allah revealed the Qur'an to his Messenger, Muhammad (saw), as guidance for the pious, a law for the Muslim, a healing for the disease that is in the hearts of those whom Allah wants to heal and a light for those whom Allah wants to give success. The chapters in this book touch upon all aspects of human existence, including matters of doctrine, social organization, and legislation.[6] It contains the fundamentals for which Allah sent the Messengers. The Qur'an was not the first book to be revealed nor was Muhammad (saw), the first Messenger to be sent. Allah has revealed the scriptures to Abraham; Torah to Moses and the Gospel to Jesus. But the contents of most of these books have been lost and have become extinct, and interpolation and alterations have entered them.

As for the Qur'an, Allah Himself guarantees its protection and makes it the witness and abolisher of earlier books. He says while addressing the Prophet (saw),

> "*And We have sent down to you [O Muhammad (saw)] the Book (this Qur'an) in truth, confirming the scripture that came before it and Muhaymin (trustworthy in highness and a witness) over it (old scriptures).*"[7]

The Qur'an guides mankind to the most righteous path in all aspects of their life and is an everlasting miracle for Muhammad (saw). It contains signs that shall abide till the day of resurrection. Allah has made the Qur'an the everlasting proof.[8]

The Prophetic Sunnah

Allah revealed the Qur'an to the Messenger and revealed to him like thereof which is the Prophetic Sunnah that explains the Qur'an. Allah has permitted him to explain the general and particular verses of the Qur'an. Allah says,

> "*And We have also sent down unto you [O Muhammad (saw)] the Dhikr [reminder and the advice (i.e. the Qur'an)] that you may explain clearly to men that is sent down to them, and that they may give thought.*"[9]

The Sunnah is the second source of the religion of Islam. It means all that is reported from the Prophet (saw)—with well-connected and authentic chain of transmitters—of his sayings, deeds and qualities. It is also a revelation from Allah to His Messenger Muhammad (saw), for the Prophet, blessings and peace be upon him, did not speak of his own desire. Allah says,

> "*Nor does he speak of (his own) desire. It is only a revelation revealed. He has been taught (this Qur'an) by one mighty in power Jibril (Gabriel).*"[10]

The Sunnah, as it is regarded as the practical implementation of Islam, it also explains the Qur'an, makes comments on it, and explains verses that have general meanings.

One must have belief in the Qur'an and the Sunnah that they are the primary sources of the religion of Islam that must be followed and turned to. The command of both must be obeyed, their prohibitions must be abstained from and their contents must be believed.

Pillars of Islam

There are five pillars of Islam (arkan-al-Islam also arkan ad-din) "pillars of the religion). The Qur'an presents them as a framework for worship and a sign of commitment to the faith. The first pillar "Shahada" is a belief and the remaining pillars are actions that a Muslim must perform to fulfil his/her obligations to Allah and the community.

First pillar is called "Shahada", it is belief that there is only one God and Muhammad (saw) is His messenger. Without this belief a person cannot be a Muslim. Muslims believe that no one has the right to be invoked, supplicated, prayed to, or shown any act of worship, but God alone. Muslims do not worship Muhammad (saw) but considers him as God's last messenger. In Qur'an, Allah describes Himself:

> "*Say, He is God, the One. God, to Whom the creatures turn for their needs. He begets not, nor was He begotten, and there is none like Him.*"[11] (Qur'an, 112:1-4).

Second pillar is "Salat" (Prayer). Muslims pray 5 times a day from sunrise to sunset: Fajr, Zuhr, Asr, Maghrib and Isha'a. Fajr is performed at dawn, Zuhr is a noon prayer, Asr is performed in the afternoon, Maghrib is the sunset prayer, and Isha is the evening prayer. Each prayer consists of a certain amount of raka'at. All of these prayers are recited while facing the Ka'bah in Mecca. Muslims must wash themselves before prayer, this washing is called Wudu. Muslims can pray at home, work or a mosque. During prayer, Muslim worship Allah and ask for His forgiveness. They also send their blessings to Prophet Muhammad (saw), Prophet Abraham (as) and their descendants.

Third pillar is "Sawm" (Fasting). Three types of fasting are recognized by the Qur'an: Ritual fasting[12], fasting as compensation for repentance (both from sura Al-Baqara), and ascetic fasting (from Al-Ahzab). Ritual fasting is an obligatory act during the month of Ramadan (Islamic lunar calendar). Muslims fast every day from morning to dusk for 29 or 30 days depending on the sighting of moon. They get up very early in the morning before sunrise and eat breakfast. Then during the day they do not eat or drink. The fast is broken at sunset called "iftar". Muslims believe that Ramadan is the month of blessings during which Qur'an was revealed to Prophet Muhammad (saw). During this month, Allah opens the gate of heaven and would forgive believers if they fast, pray, give charity and do good deeds. According to the Qu'ran:

> "*The month of Ramadan is one in which the Qur'an was revealed, as a guidance for humanity, and demonstration in the way of guidance and discrimination. So whoever among you is present should fast. If anyone is ill or on a journey, then the prescribed term is to be from other days*".[13] (Qur'an 2:185)

Fourth pillar is "Zakat'' or charity. Each adult Muslim who is gainfully employed must give two and a half per cent or more of his savings to the needy on an annual basis. In addition to zakat that is for poor people, Muslims give "sadaqah" (donations) to mosques, teaching institutions and various charity organisations. The best charity is sadaqajariya (continuous charity) e.g, teaching a skill to a person so he/she can make a living, educating people about Islam, building a school/mosque or simply planting a fruit or shade tree so that other people can benefit from it. The Prophet (saw) said, "when a person dies his/her actions come to an end except three that he/she leave behind: (1) Sadaqajariya, (2) knowledge (e.g. book) from which other derive benefit, and (3) a righteous offspring who prays for his/her forgiveness.

Fifth pillar is "Hajj". The Hajj is a pilgrimage that occurs during the Islamic month of Dhu al-Hijjah to the holy city of Mecca, and derives from an ancient Arab practice. Every able-bodied Muslim is obliged to make the pilgrimage to Mecca at least once in their lifetime if he or she can afford it.[14] When the pilgrim is around 10 km (6.2 mi) from Mecca, he must dress in Ihram clothing, which consists of two white sheets. Both men and women are required to make the pilgrimage to Mecca. The main rituals of the Hajj include walking seven times around the Kaaba, touching the black stone, travelling seven times between Mount Safa and Mount Marwa, and symbolically stoning the Devil in Mina.

Pilgrimage unites the Muslims of the World into one international fraternity.[16] The time and venue of this congress has been set by their one God. Invitation to attend is open to every Muslim. No one has the power to bar anyone. Every Muslim who attends is guaranteed full safety and freedom as long as he himself does not violate its safety.

Thus worship in Islam, whether ritual or non-ritual, trains the individual in such a way that he loves his creator most and thereby gains an unyielding will and spirit to wipe out all evil and oppression from the human society and make the word of God dominant in the World.

The Six Articles of Faith

There are certain tenets one must believe without any doubt in order to be considered a Muslim. These articles of faith are as:

Belief in Allah

This article means to believe that Allah is the one God, to whom worship is due; that He is the creator and the sustainer of everything; that it is He who gives life and causes death, and that He is Unique in His Names and Attributes.

Belief in His Angels

The angels are creations of Allah. He created them from light. They are powerful, and always do precisely as they are commanded by Allah. A Muslim must believe in the existence of angels.

Belief in His Books

Muslims believe in all of the original scriptures revealed by Allah to His Messengers. A Muslim must believe in every scripture mentioned by Allah in the Qur'an.

Belief in His Prophets and Messengers

To believe that Allah sent Messengers to His creation in order to give them glad tidings of Paradise if they believe in Allah and believe in the Messengers, and to warn them of punishment if they disobey.

Belief in the Last Day

Another article of faith is faith in the resurrection, the Last Day, the reckoning and the requital according to divine mercy and justice, as Allah says: "*Who so does an atom's weight of good shall see it; and who does an atom's weight of evil shall see it*[17]." This is his way of stirring the believer's aspiration and strengthening his resolve to take hold of himself and buckle down to acts of disobedience and good deeds.

Belief in Providence

The last of these articles is faith in Providence, both the good and the bad, the sweet and the bitter; and faith that the universe is never outside the control of the Lord's mercy, justice and wisdom. This is what causes the believer to live a life which is refined by contentment, tranquility, security and patience.

Thus, the proper belief in Allah is the essence and cornerstone of the Islamic faith. It is the key— the key to life, the key to proper living, the key to understanding reality, the key to happiness and peace. When the person truly knows Allah, he will recognize that this is what his soul has been created for and this is what it has been seeking. Once he realizes the beauty of worshipping Allah alone, he will never desire or wish to worship anyone other than Him. His soul will be a rest and his heart will be tranquil.

NOTES

1. *What is Islam—The Islamic Bulletin,* www.islamicbulletin.org.
2. *The Qur'an,* 3:84.
3. *Ibid.*, 2:177.
4. *Ibid.*, 37:4.
5. *Ibid.*, 112: 1-4.
6. *Major Sources of Islam,* https://sites.udel.edu.
7. *The Qur'an,* 5:48.
8. As-Suhaym, Muhammad bin Abdullah, *Islam: its foundation and concepts,* King Fahad National Library Cataloging-in-Publication, 2005.
9. *The Qur'an,* 16:44.
10. *Ibid.*, 53:3-5.
11. *Ibid.*, 112:1-4.
12. *Ibid.*, 2:183-187.
13. *Ibid.*, 2:185.
14. Googelberg, *Islam*, http://books.google.co.in.
15. *Ibid.*
16. *The Five Pillars of Islam,* www.Islamreligion.com.
17. *The Qur'an,* 99:7-8.

2
Education in Islam: Aims and Objectives

Noor Aisha

Introduction

The Holy Qur'an is the central religious text of Islam; which is the revelation from God (Allah). In simple words, Qur'an is the God's conversation with the whole of mankind. Qur'an is a complete instruction and guidance about how to spend a good life. It instructs to follow morality and values at every step and in every sphere of life. It encourages acquiring knowledge, which is also revealed through Hadith as: "Seek knowledge from the cradle to the grave." Also, there are various verses in the Holy Qur'an on the subject of acquiring knowledge. Even, the very first verse of the Qur'an states:

> "*Read! In the name of your Rabb; who created...who has taught [man] the use of the pen.... And taught man what he knew not.*"[1]

Qur'an talks about education in a broader and wider sense. It does not promote simply rote memorization (without understanding it); and ostentations only. Rather, according to Islam the purpose of education is to understand and adopt its ways of righteousness in conduct and in complete lifestyle. According to Qur'an, the basic purpose of education is to acquire knowledge, the knowledge which liberates you, i.e. the knowledge which abolishes your sorrows and gives you constant bliss. The aim of education according to Islam is to create attitudes which can bring improvement towards sustainable lifestyle, integral growth of human beings, and to create and develop awareness about the values. The objective of education in Islam is to give creative moral inspirations and guidance to the mankind that will enhance their understanding and application of values in their lives.

According to Qur'an, education plays a very significant role in performing the duties in a sacred manner. The concept of education inferred from the primary source of Islam i.e., Qur'an appears entirely different from that of modern education. Modern secular education divorces itself from religion as a guiding agency in every walk of life. While, Islamic education accepts the supremacy of God. But, Qur'an does not restrict to acquire worldly wisdom or knowledge; as it only instructs that every task should be done in a Qur'anic and Islamic manner.

The Holy Qur'an touches every aspect of human life[2], and it declares that Islam is a complete code of life[3], are indicative of the fact that Islamic system of education must be within the framework of Islam and Qur'an. The fundamental difference between the two systems of education is that the modern education considers its final goal as happiness in this world while Islamic education considers life, as the means to attain happiness in hereafter.[4] This simply suggests that Islamic education lays stress on hereafter and the life of this world as a preparation of hereafter. Islam demolishes the segregation of worldly and religious life. It pronounces that man is created by God; hence obedience to God in every sphere of life is a must for man. A man can secure spiritual happiness, even in this worldly life if he consciously obeys the commands of God. In this way, the first and foremost part of Islamic education is to inculcate in the minds of learners the concept of God through the absorption of His (God's) traits and qualities. The goal that Islam sets for education is to make the man obedient and grateful to God. Education is a process to instil the beliefs and ideals of Islam in the heart of the learner. Hence, the essence of education in Islam is religious. It makes man conscious of the purpose that the Holy Qur'an is the real source of knowledge and for guidance man should rely upon the Almighty.

Aims of Education in the Light of the Islam

The mind is dynamic and it has a self-adjusting and self-learning force, which suggests that the mind needs proper guidance for wholesome growth and development; and so with the Qur'anic education, as it seeks to develop the mind according to its own inherent capacities in a social environment. Qur'anic education emphasized the development of personality along with the physical, moral, intellectual, social, cultural, aesthetic and spiritual development. Thus, the aim of education is to develop individuality to the full and attain a social efficiency and dynamism, with full faith in God.

The Qur'an presents Islam as Religion[5] which is the way of life, the code of conduct. It declares that Islam is the only Truth[6] and no other way of life is just for man to follow.[7] Hence, it instructs to pray to Almighty for guidance to the straight path. Qur'an restricts of being an extremist and instructs to adopt a middle path even in the complex circumstances of life. The Qur'an conditions the faith with belief in one God and says that if anyone does not believe in one God, he would naturally go astray from the righteous (straight) path.[8] Qur'an talks about to follow middle way and a genuine path[9] of life in which man's powers, potentialities and faculties would get suitable atmosphere and congenial conditions that develops an individual harmoniously. And thus, on this way that man without going to extremes becomes able to take a balanced step in the complex situations of life. Islamic texts encourage the Muslim to be cheerful and optimistic, but not so ecstatic and carefree that they become superficial or thrill-seeking and unconcerned with serious matters in life. Islam teaches balance in thought and action. Although some practitioners may go to extremes, the religion itself does not overlook any form of extremism or radicalism and intolerance. In fact, finding the middle path is a general principle of behaviour in Islam. The Qur'an and the prophetic traditions contain specific guidelines steering people away from extremes in particular cognitive, social, and behavioural areas. Furthermore, Islam endorses socio-political and socio-economic systems that represent a balanced, middle ground.

Though there are other sources of knowledge and Islam does not deny that, it only declares that Qur'anic Revelation as the most important source of knowledge. The other sources of knowledge which the Qur'an discusses are self[10], outer world[11], Elements of Natures[12], Experience[13], History[14] i.e., Qur'an discusses about the sense organs which are the sources of acquiring empirical knowledge. Qur'an encourages to strive for knowledge and to obtain an increase in righteousness, and also it warns not to be ostentatious as it declares woe to those that strive for it to obtain an advantage over or from their fellow-believers. This all signifies that how vast and comprehensive the aims and objectives are, in Islamic system of education.

Islam is a religion in which almighty God is himself conveying his message through a book, which is a divine source of knowledge and complete guidance to the whole of mankind; hence it is never against the education of the people, rather it sets certain aims and objectives to be a perfect model of humanity; as Qur'anic education develops both the individual and society to higher and higher positions of glory of cultural and spiritual eminence.

Individual Aims of Education in Islam

The Qur'an throws light upon education from multiple angles. According to it, education in its wide meaning is acquisition of knowledge, training of mind, of the body, of the senses and emotions as well as making a man well-disciplined being that possess good manners, conduct and character. According to Qur'anic education, to purify the internal self of the individual is considered as the most important task. The sole aim of education is to bring harmony and solidarity in an individual's physical, mental, emotional and moral aspects of life is to make him able to discharge the great responsibility of God's vice-generate.[15] And to perform properly the duties and obligations of God's vice-generate it is necessary that man should be trained from his childhood and no aspect of his personality is ignored and a harmonious, integrated and balanced development of individual is achieved. During the process of education and training, the role of Islamic Faith appears very significant; this gives a spiritual direction to the whole process of education.

The aims and objectives of education evolved at the first world conference on Muslim education also corroborate the same view, that "Education should aim at the balanced growth of the total personality of Man through training of the human spirit, intellect, rational self, feelings and senses.[16] The training imparted to a Muslim must be such that faith is infused into the whole of his personality and creates in him an emotional attachment to Islam and enable him to follow the Qur'an and be governed by Islamic system of values willingly and joyfully so that he may proceed to the realization of his status as God's vice-generate to whom Almighty has promised the authority of the universe.

Societal Aims of Education in Islam

According to various educationists, the purpose of education is to develop person's individuality and expand the inherent potentialities, and to emphasize the well-being of the society is the prime aim of education. And so with the religion Islam, as it provides an ample opportunity to develop and conserve man's individuality, as it is the basic teaching of Islam that every man is individually accountable to God and no one will bear the burden of others. In addition to it, Qur'an also propounds that Islam urges to establish a just society as an aim of education.

The ultimate goal of Islam, is the idea of raising the "group or band of people", which has been explicitly mentioned in the following verse: "ye are the best of people brought up for mankind, enjoining what is right and forbidding what is wrong and believing in God."[17] Thus, it sets the goal of an Islamic society which is expected to achieve, through inculcation of Islamic education in the learner. Again the educational implication of the Holy Qur'an says, "Let there arise out of you a band of people inviting towards all which is good, enjoining what is right, and forbidding what is wrong."[18] From educational point of view this verse is very much significant as it sets the goal of Islamic society which is to disseminate knowledge. There may be various methods to discharging the duty of enjoining what is right and forbidding what is wrong; but the most powerful means to achieve this goal is education.[19]

According to Islam, the proposed educational plan is to create the real understanding of religion among the common people and to prepare them to fulfil their moral obligations and also to save them from un-Islamic ways of life. Hence, it is explicitly confirmed that "Gaining insight in religion"[20] is the prime aim of education in Islam; because only Islam and Qur'an is the book of Guidance[21] and can satisfy all the needs of developing body, mind, self, soul and spirit; and to be such a group, that call towards goodness and command what is just and forbid evil.[22]

And only that system of education will be considered Islamic which fulfils this aim. It is often misunderstood and misinterpreted that the aim of Islamic education is to acquire the knowledge of the Islamic law only; but this interpretation is incomplete in its sense. Because there is no reason to say that the aim of education in Islam is to acquire only the knowledge of religion. Rather, the aim of education according to Qur'an is to create an insight into Islam so that the learner is fully aware of the different aspects of life within Islamic system.

Thus, education in Islam is ideologically oriented and therein every scientific fact, social or natural is studied in the framework of the Islamic ideology and total view of life. According to Prophetic saying, if it is not subject to Islam it is evil, and if it becomes subject to Islam it will be great blessing to mankind. Thus, it is the duty of followers of Islam to propagate the Islamic knowledge and Islamic ways of life. As, Qur'an urges to acquire Knowledge and to practice it; also it suggests that acquire Knowledge, for the sake of Knowledge; and acquisition of knowledge for personal benefit only is not desirable in Islam; it commands that the Divine Knowledge is not for personal profit only, and the Persons who conceal the Divine Knowledge are culpable of the conjoined crime.[23] Thus in view of the above, it may be said that Qur'an keeps a collective approach towards education, and the Islamic society has a message to disseminate or publicize knowledge; and with this point in view it instructs to upbring its younger generation for the complete and all-round development.

Apprenticeship of Islamic Values

The most remarkable aspect of Islamic system of education is the aim to induce and instil higher values in the minds and hearts of the learner. If there is crisis in the value system the aims and objects of education can neither be truly determined nor properly achieved, because when values are not fixed or explicitly stated in the aims and objectives of education then there appears dissonance, because everyone is in favour of educating children but according to his own particular point of view and thus due to vagueness in the aims and objects of education, values are sometimes neglected and value-free education is adopted. But, as far as the Islamic system of education is concerned, primarily it aims at creating a pattern of behaviour on the basis of the moral philosophy of Islam. The moral values of Islam are instilled in the child's minds both by the precepts and example of the teacher and also through the educative materials designed for him. These materials whether related to natural sciences, social sciences/arts, literatures and languages—all are arranged in such a form that they might be conducive to the moral development of the child. These are to influence the inner self of the child and to inculcate in him the honest motivation of cultivating good conduct. From the Islamic point of view outward conduct is not the only important thing but the intention behind it is also considered significant.

The first step according to Islam is the moral development. The Islamic education urges to purify the intentions of the students so that they could regulate their conduct by honest motivation of earning God's pleasure. This motivation makes an individual lenient, kindhearted and of good manners. Existence of such individuals is naturally a blessing for the society as he neither misbehaves with other nor is unjust to anybody. Forgiveness and respect for others are the specific traits of his personality. He reflects in his behaviour the Godly attributes, the ideals of righteousness, goodness and beauty. Qur'an propounds qualities that are expected to be fostered in the children for developing in them a sound moral character and to constitute the moral self. The children, through the Islamic system of education, are expected to be trained in such a way that in the midst of adversity they show patience, endurance, self-governance and self-restraint. They are expected to proceed to desired objectives with faith, determination, vigour, the fear of God, and to be firm, just, steadfast, cool, calm, modest and simple and not to adopt haughtiness or arrogance, pride or hopelessness which regulates the complete behaviour of an individual. It appears from the exegesis of the Qur'an that only through this the total development of the personality can be made on the basis of the higher moral values and the young people saved from indecency, wickedness and transgression in the moral philosophy of Islam justice gets a very prominent place. Islam suggests such a moral training that enables them to respect other persons' right and with magnanimity, generosity and thankfulness to God included with love, co-operation, gratitude, sympathy, sincerity and sacrifice. Thus, the Islamic system of education is expected to inculcate the emotion of thankfulness in the younger generation. It will lead them to the goal of being generous which is considered the ultimate aim of education in Islam. The Qur'an also discusses that divine guidance is for those who perform prayer and help and pay to poor-due; and have the fear of the day of judgement day i.e., who believe in the fundamentals of Islam and shape their behaviour accordingly. These valuable precepts cover the whole aspect of character building for young people.

Conclusion

Qur'an is God's conversation with whole of humanity. Qur'an does not ask to separate our worldly life and the life of hereafter. Rather Qur'an says that present life is the preparation for the hereafter. According to education in Islam (religion) it just means to follow the God's commandments; and God's commandment is all about being a complete model of humanity. In the system of education, aims and objects is of prime importance and every component of the system serves to fulfil the aim deeply rooted in the philosophy of life. Islam demolishes the idea of segregation of secular and religious life and sets the goal of education for inculcating the beliefs and ideals of Islam in the heart and mind of the students. Education, in Islam, aims to harmonize physical, mental, emotional and moral aspects of life of an individual, in order to enable him to acquire the godly traits and shoulder the responsibility of being a perfect model of humanity. Moreover, the Islamic society as a whole accepts the responsibility of spreading the message of Islam and for this purpose upbrings its younger generation. In Islam, the ultimate aim of education is to win the pleasure of God. Its purpose is not to show ostentation or envying with the learned or disputing with the foolish or taking worldly advantages through dubious means. Education aims at inculcating Islamic values for creating in an individual an ideal of behaviour based on the moral philosophy of Islam. Learners are expected to reflect Godly virtues. Moreover, patience, fear of God, justice, generosity, thankfulness are the qualities considered essential to be inculcated in the mind and heart of the learner. Qur'an and the Prophetic traditions give instructions regarding all aspects of life: political, social, economic, material, ethical, national and international. These instructions provide us with all the details needed to perform a certain act. To summarize, Islam governs a life in all its aspects. This is the reason why it is not only a religion, but a way of life.

NOTES

1. *Surah Al-Alaq*: 1-5.
2. *Surah An'am*: 38.
3. *Surah Maida*: 3, *Surah Al-i-imran*:19.
4. *Surah Al-i-imran*:185.
5. *Surah Al-i-imran*: 19.
6. *Surah At-Tauba*: 33.
7. *Surah Az-Zumar*: 11-15.
8. *Surah Al-Fatihah*: 6.
9. *Surah Al-Baqarah*: 108, 143; *Surah Al-Maidah*: 12.
10. *Surah Al-Shams*: 7-8.
11. *Surah Al-Fatir*: 27-28.
12. *Surah Al-Baqarah*: 164.
13. *Surah Al-Balad*: 8-10.
14. *Surah Al-Asr*: 1-2.
15. *Surah Al-Baqarah*: 30.
16. Hasina Banu Ebrahim: *Early Childhood Education for Muslim Children*, p. 30.
17. *Surah Al-i-imran*: 110.
18. *Surah Al-i-imran*: 104.
19. *Surah An-Nahl*: 125.
20. *Surah At-Tauba*: 122.
21. *Surah Al-Baqarah*: 2.
22. *Surah Al-i-imran*: 104.
23. *Surah Al-Baqarah*: 159, 174.

REFERENCES

Aggarwal, J.C. (2007). *Teacher and Education in a Developing Society*, New Delhi: Vikas Publishing House.

AKC Ottaway (2013). *Education and Society*, Routledge (Taylor & Francis Group), London & New York, ISBN: 0415177545.

Hasina Banu Ebrahim (2017). *Early Childhood Education for Muslim Children: Rationales and Practices in South Africa*, Routledge (Taylor & Francis Group), London & New York.

Hassan Ali El-Najjar (2007). Mind, Self, Soul, Spirit, and Happiness, from an Islamic Perspective retrieved from http://www.aljazeerah.info/ Islamic%20Editorials/2007/November/Mind,%20self,%20Soul,%20Spirit,%20and%20Happiness%20from%20an%20Islamic%20Perspective%20By%20Hassan%20Ali%20El-Najjar.htm (accessed on 2 March, 2018)

https://www.nobleQur'an.com/translation/

Mujadad Zaman, Nadeem A. Memon (2016). *Philosophies of Islamic Education: Historical Perspectives and Emerging Discourses*, Routledge (Taylor & Francis Group), London & New York.

N.R. Swaroop Saxena, Shikha Chaturvedi (2012). *Teacher in Emerging Indian Society*, R. Lall Book Depot, Meerut, ISBN: 9789381466452.

Pearson (2012): *Teacher in Emerging Indian Society*, Pearson Series in Education, ISBN: 9788131773468.

Saeeda Shah (2015). *Education, Leadership and Islam: Theories, Discourses and Practices from an Islamic Perspective*, Routledge (Taylor & Francis Group), London & New York.

Sayyid Abul Aa'la Maududi: *Towards Understanding Islam*, Translated by Khurram Murad (2017). Markazi Maktaba Islami Publishers, New Delhi, ISBN: 8180884528.

Sayyid Abul Aa'la Maududi: *Towards Understanding the Qur'an* (Abridged Version of Tafhim al Qur'an), Translated and Edited by Zafar Ishaq Ansari, 2011.

Sayyid Muhammad Rizvi: *Education in Islam*, retrieved from https://www.al-islam.org/articles/education-in-islam-sayyid-muhammad-rizvi

3
Meaning of Life in the Context of Islam

Tariq Anwar

Introduction

As Muslims we believe in the one and only Creator Allah. He is the only One worthy of worship and has indeed created us for a purpose. He has sent many Messengers and Prophets to guide humanity to the straight path, with Muhammad (PBUH) being the Final Messenger and the Qur'an being the Final Revelation.

Allah says in the Qur'an that we were indeed created for a purpose beyond that of mere play and enjoyment. "Did you think that We had created you in play (without any purpose), and that you would not be brought back to Us?" (Qur'an 23:115)

Allah states that the reality of this life is one of deception and we should not fall for its temporary enjoyments. "Know that the life of this world is but amusement and diversion and adornment and boasting to one another and competition in increase of wealth and children – like the example of a rain whose [resulting] plant growth pleases the tillers; then it dries and you see it turned yellow; then it becomes [scattered] debris. And in the Hereafter is severe punishment and forgiveness from Allah and approval. And what is the worldly life except the enjoyment of delusion." (Qur'an 57:20)

Allah assures us that the reality of this life is that each and everyone of us is being tested, and we will be brought back to our Lord in account for every deed we have performed, both the good and the bad." [He] who created death and life to test you [as to] which of you is best in deed – and He is the Exalted in Might, the Forgiving." (Qur'an 67:2)

Allah also teaches us that the purpose of life is to also worship Him alone without associating partners with Him. This does not necessarily mean praying 24 hours a day with our face planted on the ground, but rather live our lives in obedience to God in accordance with the moral code outlined in the Qur'an. This includes being kind to your parents, relatives, neighbours, the poor and the needy. It also means fulfilling the commands of God whether it is to perform the 5 daily prayers, pay the Zakat (Charity), fast the month of Ramadan and perform the Hajj (Pilgrimage). "And I did not create the jinn and mankind except to worship Me." (Qur'an 51:56)

What is the Meaning of Life in Islam?

Life is a sacred trust from God and a human is a trustee who should handle the trust with honesty and skill, and with mindfulness of God. When God gives life He endows the human being with unique qualities and abilities, and charges the human with certain obligations. God means to help humankind fulfil the purpose of life and realize the goal of existence: to seek the pleasure of God in order to have eternal pleasure in the afterlife.

"Live in this world as if you are a traveller or a wayfarer" is a saying of the Prophet Muhammad. Life may be likened to a journey starting from a certain point and ending at a certain destination. It is a transitory stage, an introduction to the eternal life in the Hereafter.

According to Islamic teaching, the best use of life is to live it according to the guidance of God and perform good deeds in order to ensure a place in Paradise. As life is a means to an ultimate end, Islam has laid down a comprehensive system of principles and regulations on how to lead it. Muslims believe that we all belong to God and to Him is our final return. Life, therefore, is a complete circle and death is a doorway that leads to the true eternal existence.

What Is Islam?

We are providing this section for our new brothers and sisters so that they may have more information regarding the teachings of Islam; the religion of absolute submission to the one God; Allah. We sincerely hope that you will benefit from it, and that it may deepen your knowledge and increase your interest in Islam.

Although we live in the twentieth century — in probably the most secular and irreligious age in history — many of us are still inclined to stop from time to time to think about religion. And yet we find that there are so many different opinions about religion. Religions seem to cling fanatically to their own beliefs. Each in turn seems to claim that it possesses all truth, while all others are lost in hopeless error.

In an age torn by hatred, war and strife among the races, many of us look back to religion for guidance to peace and brotherhood and are disappointed when we find in most of them intolerance and narrowness of spirituality.

So, we may ask, is there a religion which teaches the Oneness of God and the oneness of mankind, and yet, at the same time is tolerant of other points of view? This is exactly the teaching of Islam. In fact, Islam teaches that this message of the Oneness of God and the brotherhood of all races is the original message which Allah sent to all prophets and religions since the dawn of human history.

However, man has changed this original teaching of Oneness and developed out of numerous mutually antagonistic sects. As Allah says in the Holy Qur'an, the revelation of Allah to Prophet Muhammad (PBUH): "And verily this Ummah of yours is a single Ummah and I am your Lord, and Cherisher: therefore fear Me (and no other). But people have cut off their affair (of unity), between them into sects: each party rejoices in that which is with itself." (Qur'an 23:52-53)

Islam still preserves this teaching of the Oneness of God and the brotherhood of all mankind. Islam seeks to implement this spirit among all races, and yet, at the same time, remains tolerant and respectful of all other heavenly religions and their followers who share the belief in the One and only God. The Holy Qur'an teaches: "Let there be no compulsion in religion: Truth stands out clear from Error: whoever rejects Tagut and believes in Allah hath grasped the most trustworthy hand-hold that never breaks. And Allah heareth and knoweth all things." (Qur'an 2:256)

The Meaning of Islam

It is false to call Islam Mohammedanism, as has been done so frequently in the West. We have already pointed out that Muslims believe that Islam is the eternal message which Allah sent to all prophets, peace be upon them, from the dawn of mankind, and not a new belief which began with the Prophet Muhammad (PBUH).

Muslims call their religion Islam, and the Arabic word Islam implies the attainment of peace through submission to Allah. The word Muslim is an adjective derived from the noun Islam, and implies one who has peace within himself from his submission to Allah.

Muslims believe in the One, Eternal God, Who created the heavens and the earth and all that exists. In Arabic, God is called Allah. There is absolutely no difference between Allah and the God of Abraham, Moses and Jesus, peace be upon them all. Muslims do not believe that Prophet Muhammad was the only Prophet; rather they believe that he was the last of the Prophets of the Old and New Testaments. The Holy Qur'an is the revealed and sacred scripture of Islam, and it teaches: "Say Ye: 'We believe in Allah and the revelation given to us, and to Abraham, Isma'il, Isaac, Jacob and the Tribes, and that given to Moses and Jesus, and that given to (all) Prophets from their Lord: We make no difference between one and another of them: and we submit to Allah.'" (Qur'an 2:136)

The Five Pillars of Islam

Islam sets down five principle duties which are obligatory upon all Muslims, and form the structure, or pillars, of his/her life. They are:

- Belief in the Oneness of Allah, and the bearing of witness to this belief by the words. "I bear witness that there is no god except Allah, and that Muhammad is His Prophet and Messenger."
- The five daily prayers at dawn, noon, afternoon, sunset and nightfall. These five daily prayers help one to develop Allah consciousness in his/her everyday life. The importance of these cannot be overemphasized. They are a constant reminder to the worshipper of the Presence and Power of Allah and help the worshipper to keep himself from deviating from the Right Path.
- The bestowal of charity on one's fellow man. Islam places great emphasis on generosity and charity as a means of purifying one's soul and getting closer to Allah. The

Muslim is enjoined to give voluntarily whenever he/she can; however, he/she is required each year to pay an obligatory charity tax of two and a half per cent of his/her annual net earnings that exceed necessities, to go to the poor and the needy, etc. The Zakat — charity — thus enables the Muslim community to take care of all its members and insures that no one will be deprived of his/her basic human right to exist.

- Fasting during the ninth month of the lunar year 'Ramadan'. This fast is enjoined upon Muslims of good health and sound body who have attained the age of physical maturity and are not prevented from performing the fast by various circumstances like travel, sickness, mental illness, or specifically in the case of women, menstruation, or childbirth. The fast of Ramadan begins at dawn and last until sunset. During this period, the Muslim abstains from eating, and drinking, sexual activity and smoking. Fasting teaches self-discipline and control, while purifying the soul and body and strengthening one's consciousness of Allah.
- The pilgrimage to Mecca. The pilgrimage is required of all Muslims at least once during their lifetime, if they have the financial means. The annual pilgrimage to Mecca is one of the greatest events of the Muslim world, uniting Muslims from every race and from every corner of the world. This is a great experience in the life of a Muslim which enables him to draw himself closer to Allah. We would like to remind the reader that the Holy Mosque in Mecca was built by Prophet Abraham and his son, the Prophet Ishmail, peace be upon them.

Who is a Muslim?

Since there is no priesthood in Islam, no clergy and no official religious institution, all one has to do to become a Muslim is to be personally convinced of the truth of what Islam teaches and bear witness that "There is no god except Allah, and that Muhammad is His Prophet."

One of the great beauties of Islam is its simplicity, its naturalness, and its lack of formalities. Islam is the religion of

Adam and of mankind in its earliest and most advanced stages of development. Allah says in the Holy Qur'an:

> "So set your face to the religion of Islam as a man by nature upright, the nature of Allah with which He has inspired mankind and molded them. There is no changing to the creation of Allah. That is the right religion, but most men know not." (Qur'an 30:30)

Some Basic Beliefs of Islam

The most fundamental concept of Islam and the backbone of all its other principles and practices is the Oneness of God—tawhiid. Islam is monotheism in its purest form, and the logic of pure monotheism is the thread which runs through the entire fabric of the Islamic way of life. Islam teaches a fundamental difference between Allah, the Creator and that which He has created. The sky, the moon, the stars, the harmony and perfection of the natural world, the grace and beauty of the human body and the excellence of the human mind, the alternation of day and night, the change of the seasons, and the mystery of life and death all point to something beyond, greater than themselves. To the believer these are all signs (ayaat) of Allah. Islam teaches that Allah is not to be likened to anything which He has created. He is All-Powerful, All-Knowing. He is beyond any imperfection, and is the fulfilment of all Perfection. He is not a substance, nor is He like any of His creatures. He is not a far away and distant God, nor is He an unapproachable ideal. He is All-Kind, All-Merciful, and All-Compassionate.

Islam teaches that Allah is eternal. He was not Himself begotten, nor has He, in turn begotten a son or a daughter. Islam rejects the concept of the incarnation of God, which is found in Hinduism, Christianity, and other religions, and believes that the concept of incarnation limits the concept of God and destroys the believer's conviction of God's Activeness and Perfection.

The Qur'an describes Allah being perfect and active:

> "Allah, there is no god except He. The Living, the Everlasting. Neither dozing nor sleep overtakes Him. To Him belongs all that is in the heavens and the earth. Who is he that shall intercede with Him except by His permission?

> He knows what will be before their hands and what was behind them. And they do not comprehend anything of His knowledge except what He willed. His Seat surrounds the heavens and earth. The preserving of them does not tire Him. He is the All High, the All-Glorious." (Qur'an 2:255)

Islam rejects the notion that Jesus (PBUH) was the son of God. Rather it honours and respects him as one of the great messengers and prophets of Allah to the Children of Israel.

Islam rejects the concept of trinity and considers it a contradiction of pure monotheism. It also rejects the argument of some Christians that God made Himself incarnate in Jesus, peace be upon him, so that God could be known by men, and also rejects the argument that Jesus, peace be upon him, died on the cross for mankind's sins. To begin with, Islam believes that man can come to know Allah and feel close to Him by means of proper prayer, fasting, charity, pilgrimage, and righteous deeds. The very practice of Islam is meant to purify the believer's soul and to bring him/her closer to Allah. With regard to the second argument, Islam teaches no human being can bear the burden of another's responsibility.

Allah is very aware of our human weaknesses and imperfection. He does not condemn us because we are created imperfect; rather He guides us to self-perfection and He forgives us and showers His Mercy upon us when we fail and then ask His forgiveness sincerely.

Muslims believe in the divine origin of the Old and New Testaments, although Muslims doubt the historical authenticity of some parts of the Old and New Testaments and do not believe them to be exact representations of what Allah originally revealed. The Qur'an upheld this view of the text of the Old and New Testaments hundreds of years ago, and in recent years, this view has been upheld by textual studies of Biblical scholars. Muslims believe in the Angels of Allah, and His Prophets, peace be upon them. They believe in the resurrection of the dead at the end of the world; they believe in the coming of the Day of Judgment and eternal life in Paradise or Hell.

Although Muslims believe that Allah is All-Powerful and maintains complete control over His creation, they also believe that Allah has created man with free will and the ability to choose and act, and that Allah is just in making man morally responsible for what man does during his/her lifetime. It is false to say that Islam teaches its followers to resign meekly and passively to whatever is their fate or destiny. Rather Islam challenges the believer to fight against wrong and oppression and to strive for the establishment of righteousness and justice.

Brotherhood and Equality of Mankind

Islam teaches that the human family is one, that there is no superiority of white over black or black over white. Islam rejects radically all notions of racial prejudice and teaches that the only basis of distinction between human beings is their individual moral qualities.

The concept of Islamic brotherhood has two primary dimensions; the relationship of Muslims to Muslims and the relationship of Muslims to non-Muslims. As for the first category Islam teaches that the brotherhood between all Muslims is to be absolute and total. The Arab has no privileges over the non-Arab, and, since there is no clergy or priesthood in Islam, all Muslims are basically equal, from top to bottom, from rich to poor, from educated to uneducated.

As for the relationships between Muslims and non-Muslims, the teaching of Islam is that this is to be a relationship of mutual respect and particularly of tolerance. It is preferable that Muslims and non-Muslims live in peace, protect each other, and cooperate with each other. As the Qur'an says: "There is no compulsion in religion." (Qur'an 2:256) and "You have your religion and I have mine." (Qur'an 109:6)

The Position of Women in Islam

Islam teaches that the woman is not inherently inferior to man; rather men and women are of similar nature. They both are equal in intellectual and spiritual capacity. Furthermore, they are both equally responsible for their deeds before Allah.

It is also true that Islam regards the woman as having a primary role to play in the constitution and running of the family. Islam places great emphasis on the role of the Muslim woman as a wife and particularly as a mother, and Muslims are often of the opinion that the best position for the woman is in the home with her children and family. However, the Muslim woman is not prohibited from leaving her home to pursue education, a teaching profession, or other worthwhile and constructive goals which profit not only her but society as well. The Qur'an establishes the spiritual equality and mutual responsibility of man and woman in verses like the following:

> "And whoever does deeds of righteousness, whether male or female, and is a believer, such will enter Paradise, and they will not be wronged even a small thing like the spot on a date-stone." (Qur'an 4:124)
> "And their Lord answered them, 'Indeed I suffer not the work of any worker, male or female, to be lost. You are equal to each other.'" (Qur'an 3:195)

The relationship of the Muslim man to his wife is not that of master to slave. Rather the entire responsibility of economic support is placed on the shoulders of the man alone and he cannot demand of his wife that she also become economically productive to support the family, although she is able to do this if she desires.

The Qur'an enunciates this responsibility of men to women in the following verse: "Men are the protectors and maintainers of women, for that Allah has preferred one over the other in bounty, and because they support them from their means. So righteous women are obedient, guarding in secret what Allah has guarded." (Qur'an 4:34)

The important point that should be made is that Islam has great respect for the woman. It does not teach that she is without a soul or that she is the root of all evil or that she is inferior to man and must be kept in seclusion and subjugation. It is also worthy of mention that the Qur'an does not teach that man fell from Paradise because of the temptation of Eve. Rather the Qur'an directs all the responsibility toward Adam himself, while adding that Allah turned to Adam in mercy and forgave him his sin. Therefore, Adam's sin stops with Adam himself, and Allah, who is the Beneficent and the Merciful, does not hold mankind responsible for the sin of Adam.

We cannot deny that the condition of women has at times been regrettable in the Muslim world, as well as in the rest of the world at large. We do not wish to justify these circumstances, but only to make the point that they did not originate from the teachings of Islam itself.

Islamic Attitude Towards War

In the eyes of some commentators on Islam in the West, Islam has been portrayed as a militant religion, a religion of blood, fire, and sword. We have already tried to draw attention to the fundamental concern of Islam for tolerance and religious freedom, and have also commented upon the emphasis Islam places on peace and cooperation among mankind. However, Islam is a practical religion, a religion which never ignores for a single moment the complexities and demands of the harsh realities and facts of life.

Islam is fundamentally concerned with establishing societies in which the rights of freedom of belief, human rights, and protection of life, dignity, and property are secure from both internal and external threats. Therefore, Islam teaches its followers to be merciful and inclined toward forgiveness and peace even in times of war.

Islam therefore stipulates principles which Muslims are to follow before, during, and after war. Peace is to be established on the basis of justice. Muslims are not to be aggressive or to violate treaties which they have concluded with others, but war is to be waged in defense of the Muslim community and what it stands for. During war, there is to be no killing of civilians and those who do no participate directly in the war. Prisoners are to be treated humanely. Destruction of lands, fruit trees, animals, and towns and villages is to be avoided. Muslims are to be inclined to peace if the enemy is truthfully inclined to peace, and they are to make treaties and agreements to preserve that peace and then observe those treaties as long as the enemy observes them. The concept of 'jihad' is one of the highest concepts in Islam. The term has at times been translated as 'Holy War'. However, this translation is incomplete for Jihad also means by language 'struggling'. It is a concept which places great emphasis on activism and self-sacrifice, although it does not apply to sacrifice in war alone. The Prophet (PBUH) said that the greatest jihad is the striving of the Muslim to purify himself. The lesser jihad consists of all the striving the Muslim does in his external life, charity, righteous living and acts, the constant effort to achieve the Right Path in his dealings with his fellow men. This is true striving in the Way of Allah.

Faith in Action

Faith without action is a dead letter. Islam teaches us that faith by itself is not enough until it is transformed into action. The Prophet Muhammad (PBUH) said: "Faith does not depend on raising hopes, but it is something which is firmly established in the heart and testified to by action. Indeed, there are people who have been deceived by their hopes, so that they finally leave this world without merit. They used to say, 'We have good expectations from Allah.' Yet they only deceived themselves. For had they truly placed good expectations in Allah, they would have excelled in good deeds."

Each Muslim is taught that he/she is personally responsible for his/her own actions, both in this world and in the hereafter. Islam teaches that every individual must carry the responsibility of his/her own actions and that no one can carry that burden for them.

The Benefit of Embracing Islam

Among the many benefits of embracing Islam are that once you bear witness that: "There is no god except Allah, and Muhammad is His Prophet", all your past sins are forgiven and all your past sins are transformed into merits! You also receive the reward of believing the religion of the Prophet Jesus, if you are a Christian, or Prophet Moses, if you are a Jew, and the religion of Prophet Muhammad, which means that you receive two rewards.

Conclusion

From the above descriptions we are bound to conclude that Muslims consider their religion to be very rational and consistent with the dictates of the believing and reasoning mind. Furthermore, the Qur'an teaches that the rational faculty is one of the greatest gifts of Allah to man, and it encourages us to use this faculty and to develop it. Islam does not ask its followers to believe and then follow everything blindly and unquestioningly. The Qur'an says, for instance: "And if you are in doubt about what we have send down to our worshipper, then bring a chapter like it, and call your witnesses besides Allah, if you are truthful." (Qur'an 2:23)

Islam encourages reasoning, thought and personal opinion. The Prophet (PBUH) said: "The differences of opinion among the learned of my followers are Allah's mercy." Islam has great respect for learning science and for man's exploration of the secrets of nature and of creation. In fact Allah challenges man on many occasions in the Qur'an to deepen his faith, knowledge, and wisdom from study and contemplation of the natural world, its harmony, symmetry, and beauty. For example: "He it is who created the seven heavens in harmony. Never can you see a lack of symmetry in the creation of the Compassionate. So look yet again, can you perceive any flaw? Then look again, and still another time; your vision will return unto you weakened and dim." (Qur'an 67:3-4)

The individual capacities and unique abilities of people are a gift of Allah, to be developed, perfected, and used for the benefit of humanity. Islam does not try to crush the individuality of its believers, but rather to guide each believer to perfection and purify his own uniqueness. This multiplicity of expressive and developed personalities enriches society and places it on a higher level, like the beauty of an intricate but unified arabesque.

REFERENCES

file:///C:/Users/%23mE/Desktop/What is the purpose of human life in Islam _ Muslim Converts' Association of Singapore.htm

file:///C:/Users/%23mE/Desktop/What Is Islam : The Meaning of Islam, Some Basic Beliefs of Islam.htm

file:///C:/Users/%23mE/Desktop/Islam%20_%20Inspired%20by%20Muhammad.htm

file:///C:/Users/%23mE/Desktop/The%20Purpose%20of%20Life%20_%20IT'S%20TIME%20FOR%20ISLAM%20TO%20DO%20THE%20TALKING%20_%20ONE%20MESSAGE%20_%20ONE%20GOD%20_%20IT'S%20TIME%20FOR%20ISLAM%20TO%20DO%20THE%20TALKING.htm

4

Education in Islam

Mohd Zubair Kales

Education in Islam is a concept based on verses of the Qur'an as well as Hadiths that emphasize the positive benefits to be gained from the acquisition of knowledge. In Arabic three terms are used for education. The most common is *ta'līm*, from the root *'alima*, which means knowing, being aware, perceiving and learning. Another term is *Tarbiyah* from the root of *raba*, which means spiritual and moral growth based on the will of God. The third term is *Ta'dīb* from the root *aduba* which means to be cultured or refined in social behaviour.

Syed Muhammad Naquib al-Attas described the Islamic purpose of education as a balanced growth of the total personality through training the spirit, intellect, rational self, feelings and bodily senses such that faith is infused into the whole personality.

Seyyed Hossein Nasr stated that, while education does prepare humankind for happiness in this life, "Its ultimate goal is the abode of permanence and all education points to the permanent world of eternity".

According to the Nahj al-Balagha, there are two kinds of knowledge: knowledge merely heard and that which is absorbed. The former has no benefit unless it is absorbed. The heard knowledge is gained from the outside and the other is absorbed knowledge means the knowledge that rose from nature and human disposition, referred to the power of innovation of a person. The Qur'an is the optimal source of knowledge. For teaching Qur'anic traditions, the Maktab as elementary school emerged in mosques, private homes, shops, tents, and even outside.

Islam—History of Islamic Education, Aims and Objectives of Islamic Education

Islam has, from its inception, placed a high premium on education and has enjoyed a long and rich intellectual tradition. Knowledge (*'ilm*) occupies a significant position within Islam, as evidenced by the more than 800 references to it in Islam's most revered book, the Koran. The importance of education is repeatedly emphasized in the Koran with frequent injunctions, such as "God will exalt those of you who believe and those who have knowledge to high degrees" (58:11), "O my Lord! Increase me in knowledge" (20:114) and "As God has taught him, so let him write" (2:282). Such verses provide a forceful stimulus for the Islamic community to strive for education and learning.

Islamic education is uniquely different from other types of educational theory and practice largely because of the all-encompassing influence of the Koran. The Koran serves as a comprehensive blueprint for both the individual and society and as the primary source of knowledge. The advent of the Koran in the seventh century was quite revolutionary for the predominantly illiterate Arabian society. Arab society had enjoyed a rich oral tradition, but the Koran was considered the word of God and needed to be organically interacted with by means of reading and reciting its words. Hence, reading and writing for the purpose of accessing the full blessings of the Koran was an aspiration for most Muslims. Thus, education in Islam unequivocally derived its origins from a symbiotic relationship with religious instruction.

History of Islamic Education

Thus, in this way, Islamic education began. Pious and learned Muslims (*mu'allim* or *mudarris*), dedicated to making the teachings of the Koran more accessible to the Islamic community, taught the faithful in what came to be known as the *kuttāb* (plural, *katātīb*). The *kuttāb* could be located in a variety of venues: mosques, private homes, shops, tents, or even out in the open. Historians are uncertain as to when the *katātīb* were first established, but with the widespread desire of the faithful to study the Koran, *katātīb* could be found in virtually every part of the Islamic empire by the middle of the eighth century. The *kuttāb* served a vital social function as the only vehicle for formal public instruction for primary-age children and continued so until Western models of education were introduced in the modern period. Even at present, it has exhibited remarkable durability and continues to be an important means of religious instruction in many Islamic countries.

The curriculum of the *kuttāb* was primarily directed to young male children, beginning as early as age four, and was centred on Koranic studies and on religious obligations such as ritual ablutions, fasting, and prayer. The focus during the early history of Islam on the education of youth reflected the belief that raising children with correct principles was a holy obligation for parents and society. As Abdul Tibawi wrote in 1972, the mind of the child was believed to be "like a white clean paper, once anything is written on it, right or wrong, it will be difficult to erase it or superimpose new writing upon it" (p. 38). The approach to teaching children was strict, and the conditions in which young students learned could be quite harsh. Corporal punishment was often used to correct laziness or imprecision. Memorization of the Koran was central to the curriculum of the *kuttāb,* but little or no attempt was made to analyze and discuss the meaning of the text. Once students had memorized the greater part of the Koran, they could advance to higher stages of education, with increased complexity of instruction. Western analysts of the *kuttāb* system usually criticize two areas of its pedagogy: the limited range of subjects taught and the exclusive reliance on memorization. The contemporary *kuttāb* system still emphasizes memorization and recitation as important means of learning. The value placed on memorization during students' early religious training directly influences their approaches to learning when they enter formal education offered by the modern state. A common frustration of modern educators in the Islamic world is that while their students can memorize copious volumes of notes and textbook pages, they often lack competence in critical analysis and independent thinking.

During the golden age of the Islamic empire (usually defined as a period between the tenth and thirteenth centuries), when western Europe was intellectually backward and stagnant, Islamic scholarship flourished with an impressive openness to the rational sciences, art, and even literature. It was during this period that the Islamic world made most of its contributions to the scientific and artistic world. Ironically, Islamic scholars preserved much of the knowledge of the Greeks that had been prohibited by the Christian world. Other outstanding contributions were made in areas of chemistry, botany, physics, mineralogy, mathematics, and astronomy, as many Muslim thinkers regarded scientific truths as tools for accessing religious truth.

Gradually, the open and vigorous spirit of enquiry and individual judgment (*ijtihād*) that characterized the golden age gave way to a more insular, unquestioning acceptance (*taqlīd*) of the traditional corpus of authoritative knowledge. By the thirteenth century, according to Aziz Talbani, the '*ulama*' (religious scholars) had become "self-appointed interpreters and guardians of religious knowledge.... learning was confined to the transmission of traditions and dogma, and [was] hostile to research and scientific inquiry" (p. 70). The mentality of *taqlīd* reigned supreme in all matters, and religious scholars condemned all other forms of inquiry and research. Exemplifying the *taqlīd* mentality, Burhän al-Din al-Zarnüji wrote during the thirteenth century, "Stick to ancient things while avoiding new things" and "Beware of becoming engrossed in those disputes which come about after one has cut loose from the ancient authorities" (pp. 28, 58). Much of what was written after the thirteenth century lacked originality, and it consisted mostly of commentaries on existing canonical works without adding any substantive new ideas. The lethal combination of *taqlīd* and foreign invasion beginning in the thirteenth century served to dim Islam's preeminence in both the artistic and scientific worlds.

Despite its glorious legacy of earlier periods, the Islamic world seemed unable to respond either culturally or educationally to the onslaught of Western advancement by the eighteenth century. One of the most damaging aspects of European colonialism was the deterioration of indigenous cultural norms through secularism. With its veneration of human reason over divine revelation and its insistence on separation of religion and state, secularism is anathema to Islam, in which all aspects of life, spiritual or temporal, are interrelated as a harmonious whole. At the same time, Western institutions of education, with their pronounced secular/religious dichotomy, were infused into Islamic countries in order to produce functionaries to feed the bureaucratic and administrative needs of the state. The early modernizers did not fully realize the extent to which secularized education fundamentally conflicted with Islamic thought and traditional lifestyle. Religious education was to remain a separate and personal responsibility, having no place in public education. If Muslim students desired religious training, they could supplement their existing education with moral instruction in traditional religious schools—the *kuttāb*. As a consequence, the two differing education systems evolved independently with little or no official interface.

Aims and Objectives of Islamic Education

The Arabic language has three terms for education, representing the various dimensions of the educational process as perceived by Islam. The most widely used word for education in a formal sense is *ta'līm,* from the root *'alima* (to know, to be aware, to perceive, to learn), which is used to denote knowledge being sought or imparted through instruction and teaching. *Tarbiyah,* from the root *raba* (to increase, to grow, to rear), implies a state of spiritual and ethical nurturing in accordance with the will of God. *Ta'dīb,* from the root *aduba* (to be cultured, refined, well-mannered), suggests a person's development of sound social behaviour. What is meant by *sound* requires a deeper understanding of the Islamic conception of the human being.

Education in the context of Islam is regarded as a process that involves the complete person, including the rational, spiritual, and social dimensions. As noted by Syed Muhammad al-Naquib al-Attas in 1979, the comprehensive and integrated approach to education in Islam is directed toward the "balanced growth of the total personality...through training Man's spirit, intellect, rational self, feelings and bodily senses...such that faith is infused into the whole of his personality" (p. 158). In Islamic educational theory, knowledge is gained in order to actualize and perfect all dimensions of the human being. From an Islamic perspective, the highest and most useful model of perfection is the prophet Muhammad, and the goal of Islamic education is that people be able to live as he lived. Seyyed Hossein Nasr wrote in 1984 that while education does prepare humankind for happiness in this life, "its ultimate goal is the abode of permanence and all education points to the permanent world of eternity" (p. 7). To ascertain truth by reason alone is restrictive, according to Islam, because spiritual and temporal realities are two sides of the same sphere. Many Muslim educationists argue that favouring reason at the expense of spirituality interferes with balanced growth. Exclusive training of the intellect, for example, is inadequate in developing and refining elements of love, kindness, compassion, and selflessness, which have an altogether spiritual ambiance and can be engaged only by processes of spiritual training.

Education in Islam is twofold: acquiring intellectual knowledge (through the application of reason and logic) and developing spiritual knowledge (derived from divine revelation and spiritual experience). According to the worldview of Islam, provision in education must be made equally for both. Acquiring knowledge in Islam is not intended as an end but as a means to stimulate a more elevated moral and spiritual consciousness, leading to faith and righteous action.

Importance of Education in Islam

Islam is the religion of peace, and it is one of the most sacred and trustworthy religions, which has given us guidance in every aspect of life. Islam has given us education with knowledge which has no limits. The Holy Qur'an is the most sacred book of Allah revealed on Prophet Muhammad (SAW), for the upliftment, guidance and enriched messages to the humanity.

Education is the knowledge of putting one's potentials to maximum use. Without education, no one can find the proper right path in this world.

This importance of education is basically for two reasons. Education makes man a right thinker. Without education, no one can think properly in an appropriate context. It tells man how to think and how to make decision. The second reason for the importance of education is that only through the attainment of education; man is enabled to receive information from the external world. It is well said that:

> "Without education, man is as though in a closed room and with education he finds himself in a room with all its windows open towards outside world."

This is why Islam attaches such great importance to knowledge and education. When the Qur'an began to be revealed, the first word of its first verse was 'Iqra' that is, read.

The reflective book of Holy Qur'an is so rich in content and meaning that if the history of human thought continues forever, this book is not likely to be read to its end. Every day it conveys a new message to the humanity. Every morning, it gives us new thoughtful ideas and bound us in the boundaries of ethics.

Islamic Education is one of the best systems of education, which makes an ethical groomed person with all the qualities, which he/she should have as a human being. The Western world has created the wrong image of Islam in the world. They don't know that our teachings are directly given to us from Allah, who is the creator of this world, through our Prophets.

The Muslims all-over the world are thirsty of acquiring quality education. They know their boundaries and never try to cross it. It is the West, which has created a hype that the Muslim are not in a path of getting proper education. They think that our education teaches us fighting, about weapons, etc., which is so false. This is true that there are certain elements, which force an individual to be on the wrong path, because as we will mould a child, they will be like that, but it doesn't mean that our religion teaches improperly to us.

Our Holy Prophet (SAW), said,

Seek knowledge from the cradle to the grave.

and:

Seek knowledge even if it is to be found in a place as distant as China. At the battle of Badr, in which our beloved Holy Prophet (SAW) gained victory over his foes, seventy people of the enemy rank were taken to prison. These prisoners were literate people. In order to benefit from their education, the Prophet declared that if one prisoner teaches ten Muslim children how to read and write, this will serve as his ransom and he will be set free. This was the first school in the history of Islam established by the Prophet himself with all its teachers being non-Muslims. The Sunnah of the Prophet shows that education is to be received whatever the risk involved.

Today, the Muslims are acquiring good ideas, thoughts, knowledge, and skills, from all corners of the world. The world is moving very fast, and in this industrialized world, it is the duty of the teachers to give quality ethical integrated education to the Muslim students worldwide, because children are invaluable assets of future generations.

The Prophet Muhammad (SAW) encouraged all Muslims to acquire knowledge and share it. He said:

> "Acquire knowledge, for he who acquires it in the way of Allah performs an act of piety; he who speaks of it, praises the Lord; he who seeks it, adores Allah; he who dispenses instruction in it, bestows alms; and he who imparts it to others, performs an act of devotion to Allah." (Bukhari, Muslim)

All the teachers of either secular or religious education should give more attention to the pupils inside the classroom. It is necessary that in the Islamic system that we should consider these dear children as our own children, and put aside all other considerations, and rise above all such things and realize our duty and our mission. We should raise the standards of education and attend to the needs of these children. We should realize our duties with earnestness and awaken to the sense of responsibility. It has been seen that there are certain teachers who are not fulfilling their duties with keen interest. I would like to request all the teachers that for the sake of God, for the sake of your revolutionary duty, teach the children with devotion and dedication.

It is important that we advance our work through discussions, debates, studies, and through proper distribution of work among ourselves. We must never forget that we are living in an Islamic State, and our aim should be simultaneously to create both an independent as well as an Islamic culture in character. Independence and richness of content are indeed among the characteristics of the Islamic culture. Our system is an ideological system.

We should make our child enthusiastic, dynamic, and this search should pervade every corner of our society. We should aspire them to be truthful and sincere.

Self-sacrifice and generosity, love of freedom, the resolve for resistance and headstrong perseverance, the courage to welcome martyrdom—all these are the new values of the new generation, which should be taught according to the teaching of Islam.

The doors of the school should always be kept open for the sake of Islam, for the sake of the Muslim Ummah.

Aims and Purposes of Muslim Education

Islam placed a high value on education, and, as the faith spread among diverse peoples, education became an important channel through which to create a universal and cohesive social order. By the middle of the 9th century, knowledge was divided into three categories: the Islamic sciences, the philosophical and natural sciences (Greek knowledge), and the literary arts. The Islamic sciences, which emphasized the study of the Qur'ān (the Islamic scripture) and the Hadīth (the sayings and traditions of the Prophet Muhammad) and their interpretation by leading scholars and theologians, were valued the most highly, but Greek scholarship was considered equally important, albeit less virtuous.

Early Muslim education emphasized practical studies, such as the application of technological expertise to the development of irrigation systems, architectural innovations, textiles, iron and steel products, earthenware, and leather products; the manufacture of paper and gunpowder; the advancement of commerce; and the maintenance of a merchant marine. After the 11th century, however, denominational interests dominated higher learning, and the Islamic sciences achieved preeminence. Greek knowledge was studied in private, if at all, and the literary arts diminished in significance as educational policies encouraging academic freedom and new learning were replaced by a closed system characterized by an intolerance toward scientific innovations, secular subjects, and creative scholarship. This denominational system spread throughout eastern Islam from Transoxania (roughly, modern-day Tajikistan, Uzbekistan, and south-west Kazakhstan) to Egypt, with some 75 schools in existence between about 1050 and 1250.

Organization of Education

The system of education in the Muslim world was unintegrated and undifferentiated. Learning took place in a variety of institutions, among them the *ḥalqah,* or study circle; the *maktab* (*kuttab*), or elementary school; the palace schools; bookshops and literary salons; and the various types of colleges, the *meshed,* the *masjid,* and the madrasa. All the schools taught essentially the same subjects.

The simplest type of early Muslim education was offered in the mosques, where scholars who had congregated to discuss the Qur'ān began before long to teach the religious sciences to interested adults. Mosques increased in number under the caliphs, particularly the Abbāsids: 3,000 of them were reported in Baghdad alone in the first decade of the 10th century; as many as 12,000 were reported in Alexandria in the 14th century, most of them with schools attached. Some mosques—such as that of al-Manṣūr, built during the reign of Hārūn al-Rashīd in Baghdad, or those in Isfahan, Mashhad, Ghom, Damascus, Cairo, and the Alhambra (Granada)—became centres of learning for students from all-over the Muslim world. Each mosque usually contained several study circles (*ḥalqah*), so named because the teacher was, as a rule, seated on a dais or cushion with the pupils gathered in a semicircle before him. The more advanced a student, the closer he was seated to the teacher. The mosque circles varied in approach, course content, size, and quality of teaching, but the method of instruction usually emphasized lectures and memorization. Teachers were, as a rule, looked upon as masters of scholarship, and their lectures were meticulously recorded in notebooks. Students often made long journeys to join the circle of a great teacher. Some circles, especially those in which the Ḥadīth was studied, were so large that it was necessary for assistants to repeat the lecture so that every student could hear and record it.

Elementary schools (*maktab,* or *kuttab*), in which pupils learned to read and write, date to the pre-Islamic period in the Arab world. After the advent of Islam, these schools developed into centres for instruction in elementary Islamic subjects. Students were expected to memorize the Qur'an as perfectly as possible. Some schools also included in their curriculum the study of poetry, elementary arithmetic, penmanship, ethics (manners), and elementary grammar. *Maktab*s were quite common in almost every town or village in the Middle East, Africa, Sicily, and Spain.

Schools conducted in royal palaces taught not only the curriculum of the *maktab*s but also social and cultural studies designed to prepare the pupil for higher education, for service in the government of the caliphs, or for polite society. The instructors were called *mus'addib*, or instructors in good manners. The exact content of the curriculum was specified by the ruler, but oratory, history, tradition, formal ethics, poetry, and the art of good conversation were often included. Instruction usually continued long after the pupils had passed elementary age.

The high degree of learning and scholarship in Islam, particularly during the Abbāsid period in eastern Islam and the later Umayyads in western Islam, encouraged the development of bookshops, copyists, and book dealers in large, important Islamic cities such as Damascus, Baghdad, and Córdoba. Scholars and students spent many hours in these bookshop schools browsing, examining, and studying available books or purchasing favourite selections for their private libraries. Book dealers travelled to famous bookstores in search of rare manuscripts for purchase and resale to collectors and scholars and thus contributed to the spread of learning. Many such manuscripts found their way to private libraries of famous Muslim scholars such as Avicenna, al-Ghazālī, and al-Fārābī, who in turn made their homes centres of scholarly pursuits for their favourite students.

Fundamental to Muslim education though the circle schools, the *maktab*s, and the palace schools were, they embodied definite educational limitations. Their curricula were limited; they could not always attract well-trained teachers; physical facilities were not always conducive to a congenial educational environment; and conflicts between religious and secular aims in these schools were almost irreconcilable. Most importantly, these schools could not meet the growing need for trained personnel or provide sufficient educational opportunities for those who wished to continue their studies. These pressures led to the creation of a new type of school, the madrasa, which became the crown and glory of medieval Muslim education. The madrasa was an outgrowth of the *masjid,* a type of mosque college dating to the 8th century. The differences between these two institutions are still being studied, but most scholars believe that the *masjid* was also a place of worship and that, unlike the madrasa, its endowment supported only the faculty and not the students as well. A third type of college, the *meshed* (shrine college), was usually a madrasa built next to a pilgrimage centre. Whatever their particularities, all three types of colleges specialized in legal instruction, each turning out experts in one of the four schools of Sunni, or orthodox, Islamic law.

Madrasas may have existed as early as the 9th century, but the most famous one was founded in 1057 by the vizier Niẓām al-Mulk in Baghdad. The Niẓāmīyah, devoted to Sunni learning, served as a model for the establishment of an extensive network of such institutions throughout the eastern Islamic world, especially in Cairo, which had 75 madrasas; in Damascus, which had 51; and in Aleppo, where the number of madrasas rose from 6 to 44 between 1155 and 1260.

Important institutions also developed in western Islam, under the Umayyads, in the Spanish cities of Córdoba, Sevilla (Seville), Toledo, Granada, Murcia, Almería, Valencia, and Cádiz. The madrasas had no standard curriculum; the founder of each school determined the specific courses that would be taught, but they generally offered instruction in both the religious sciences and the physical sciences.

The contribution of these institutions to the advancement of knowledge was vast. Muslim scholars calculated the angle of the ecliptic; measured the size of the Earth; calculated the precession of the equinoxes; explained, in the field of optics and physics, such phenomena as refraction of light, gravity, capillary attraction, and twilight; and developed observatories for the empirical study of heavenly bodies. They made advances in the uses of drugs, herbs, and foods for medication; established hospitals with a system of interns and externs; discovered causes of certain diseases and developed correct diagnoses of them; proposed new concepts of hygiene; made use of anesthetics in surgery with newly innovated surgical tools; and introduced the science of dissection in anatomy. They furthered the scientific breeding of horses and cattle; found new ways of grafting to produce new types of flowers and fruits; introduced new concepts of irrigation, fertilization, and soil cultivation; and improved upon the science of navigation. In the area of chemistry, Muslim scholarship led to the discovery of such substances as potash, alcohol, nitrate of silver, nitric acid, sulfuric acid, and mercury chloride. It also developed to a high degree of perfection the arts of textiles, ceramics, and metallurgy.

Major Periods of Muslim Education and Learning

The renaissance of Islamic culture and scholarship developed largely under the Abbāsid administration in eastern Islam and later under the Umayyads in western Islam, mainly in Spain, between 800 and 1000. This latter period, the golden age of Islamic scholarship, was largely a period of translation and interpretation of Classical thoughts and their adaptation to Islamic theology and philosophy. The period also witnessed the introduction and assimilation of Hellenistic, Persian, and Hindu mathematics, astronomy, algebra, trigonometry, and medicine into Muslim culture.

Whereas the 8th and 9th centuries—mainly between 750 and 900—were characterized by the introduction of Classical learning and its refinement and adaptation to Islamic culture, the 10th and 11th were centuries of interpretation, criticism, and further adaptation. There followed a period of modification and significant additions to Classical culture through Muslim scholarship. Creative scholarship in Islam from the 10th to the 12th century included works by such scholars as Omar Khayyam, al-Bīrūnī, Fakhr al-Dīn al-Rāzī, Avicenna (Ibn Sīnā), al-Ṭabarī, Avempace (Ibn Bājjah), and Averroës (Ibn Rushd). During the 12th and 13th centuries, most of the works of Classical learning and the creative Muslim additions were translated from Arabic into Hebrew and Latin. These translations were instrumental in bringing about the early phases of the European intellectual awakening, which coincided with the decline of Muslim scholarship.

Influence of Islamic learning on the West

As Europe was absorbing the fruits of Islam's centuries of creative productivity, signs of Latin Christian awakening were evident throughout the European continent. The 12th century was one of intensified traffic of Muslim learning into the Western world through many hundreds of translations of Muslim works, which helped Europe seize the initiative from Islam when political conditions in Islam brought about a decline in Muslim scholarship. By 1300, European scholars stood once again on the solid ground of Hellenistic thought, enriched or modified through Muslim and Byzantine efforts.

Mehdi K. Nakosteen
Joseph S. Szyliowicz

REFERENCES

Abdullah, Abdul-Rahman Salih. 1982. *Educational Theory: A Qur'anic Outlook.* Makkah, Saudi Arabia: Umm al-Qura University Press.

Al-Alawni, Taha J. 1991. "*Taql Āīd* and the Stagnation of the Muslim Mind." *American Journal of Islamic Social Sciences*, 8:513–524.

Ali, Syed Ausef. 1987. "Islam and Modern Education." *Muslim Education Quarterly*, 4 (2):36–44.

Al-Attas, Syed Muhammad Al-Naquib. 1979. *Aims and Objectives of Islamic Education*. Jeddah, Saudi Arabia: Hodder and Stoughton.

Al-Attas, Syed Muhammad Al-Naquib. 1985. *Islam, Secularism, and the Philosophy of the Future*. London: Mansell.

Al-Zarnüji, Burhän Al-Din. 1947. *Ta'alim al-Muta'allim: Tariq al-Ta'allum* (Instruction of the student: The method of learning), trans. Gustave Edmund von Grunebaum and Theodora M. Abel. New York: Kings Crown Press.

Cook, Bradley J. 1999. "Islamic versus Western Conceptions of Education: Reflections on Egypt." *International Review of Education*, 45:339–357.

Dodge, Bayard. 1962. *Muslim Education in Medieval Times*. Washington, DC: Middle East Institute.

Husain, Syed Sajjad, and Ashraf, Syed Ali. 1979. *Crisis in Muslim Education*. Jeddah, Saudi Arabia: Hodder and Stoughton.

Landau, Jacob M. 1986. "*Kutta Åb.*" In *Encyclopedia of Islam*. Leiden, Netherlands: E.J. Brill.

Makdisi, George. 1981. *The Rise of Colleges: Institutions of Learning in Islam and the West*. Edinburgh: Edinburgh University Press.

Nasr, Seyyed Hossein. 1984. "The Islamic Philosophers' Views on Education." *Muslim Education Quarterly*, 2 (4):5–16.

Shalaby, Ahmed. 1954. *History of Muslim Education*. Beirut, Lebanon: Dar al-Kashaf.

Talbani, Aziz. 1996. "Pedagogy, Power, and Discourse: Transformation of Islamic Education." *Comparative Education Review*, 40 (1):66–82.

Tibawi, Abdul Latif. 1972. *Islamic Education*. London: Luzac.

Bradley J. Cook. Read more: Islam—History of Islamic Education, Aims and Objectives of Islamic Education—Knowledge, Religious, Koran, and Spiritual—State University.comhttp://education.stateuniversity.com/pages/2133/Islam.html#ixzz5GfhYXJ00

5
Islam, Education and Curriculum

Shaikh Haroon Moinuddin and *Hussein Ahmed Abdo Rajhy*

Introduction

The purpose of Islamic education is giving meaning to life and enriching it with the light of the Islamic faith as outlined in the Qur'an. Another purpose is strengthening and advancing human societies. "Ethical education is one of the first and foremost objectives of all religions including the religion of Islam. Besides its ethical and moral teachings that are meant to provide man with a sound and perfect belief system, Islam offers man both a theoretical and a practical programme for education and moral training and fresh interpretations of these teachings can prove to be very beneficial for the present day human society", Noaparast, B.K. (2001:2).

The term "Islamic education" means education in the light of Islam itself, which is rooted in the teachings of the Qur'an – the holy book of Muslims. Panjwani Farid (2004) observed that there is a diversity of approaches to, and stances taken on, writings about Islam and education. While a vast majority of this literature is based on the view that there is a distinct Islamic position with regard to education, some critical voices question this fundamental assumption. The advocates of a distinctively Islamic approach to education also differ among themselves on various matters; some argue for a common inter-faith religious framework on education, while others claim, at least implicitly, a superiority of the Islamic approach over those of other religions.

A contemporary discussion on Islam and education usually begins with a critique of the impact of Western and Western-based educational systems on the Muslim societies and the societies that have a significant Muslim population. Panjwani Farid (2004) Because of the controversial debate on the adaptation of the Western educational system, Muslim theorists have adopted two basic approaches to modern knowledge. The first approach holds that the acquisition of modern knowledge should be limited to only practical technological sphere because Western traditions of knowledge might create doubt in the Muslim mind. The second approach advocates that Muslims can and should acquire Western scientific and intellectual traditions because knowledge itself cannot be harmful. Anwaruddin S.M. (2012).

The philosophy of Islamic education has changed itself by passing through different ages. It has brought about both theoretical and practical changes in the system of education from time to time. "As Islam reached other lands, Muslim education took its root and developed, adopting the pre-existing system of education; educational traditions of those civilizations left a permanent imprint on the Muslim system of education". Daun H. and Arjmand R. (2018). This has affected not only the aims and objectives of education, but the techniques of curriculum transaction and organizational aspects also. A glimpse of the history of education through ages would reveal this fact. Abdul Waheedu K. (2003:2-3)

Islamic Education and Approaches to Acquisition

'Islam and education' is a strand within the trend of relating the idea of Islam to other social, political and intellectual ideas. In this sense, the discourse is a part of a widely advocated call for the Islamization of various aspects of society—economics, knowledge and science, politics, etc. Panjwani Farid (2004)

The Arabic word 'tarbiyah', as an equivalent term to education, is widely used to indicate the plan of Islam in shaping the humans. The word 'tarbiyah', with regard to its Arabic root, means preparation for enhancement and growth and, hence, is used to indicate feeding the baby. However, it is, in addition, used to indicate purification ('tahzyb') which means to dismiss bad moral characteristics. In this case, it is meant that moral purification leads to an enhancement in spiritual position and, hence purification could be called 'tarbiyah'. Noaparast, B.K. (2001:2)

Muslims have always placed a high premium value on education. Islamic education through the teaching and learning of the Qur'an can be traced back to the Prophet Muhammad's time. Subsequently, informal religious instruction took place in sites such as mosques, palaces and homes of learned people, culminating in organized educational institutions of Kuttabs and Madrasahs, in the eleventh century. Tan Charlene (2014)

Education conceived of, in Islamic terms, seeks to provide a sense of spirituality derived from one's own Islamic traditions, while at the same time empowering students to reflect, inquire and collaborate with others Islamic educational institutions have evolved, adapted and transformed themselves in response to changing needs, circumstances and times. The result today is a tapestry of Islamic educational institutions across regions, each with its own origin, trajectory and stories of aspirations, success and struggles. Tan Charlene (2014)

The rich diversity within Islamic education should not surprise us, considering that Islam is not just a religious system but also a *cultural* system. The two senses are, of course, not mutually exclusive although they emphasize different aspects of the faith. The former underscores Islam as fundamentally comprising shared foundational doctrines held by Muslims; the very word 'Islam' comes from the Arabic word *al-Islam* that means 'surrender' as well as the peace that issues from one's surrender to God. Islam as a cultural system, on the other hand, stresses the practical applications of Islam through different kinds of social groupings such as *tariqah* (ways of life) and *ahl* (people, relations). Islam encompasses complex networks of cognitive and behavioural dispositions that are political, religious, moral, epistemological and aesthetic in nature. It is always in flux, and is therefore placed in a historical and social context. Tan Charlene (2014)

Islamic Knowledge and Approaches to Acquisition

Acquisition of knowledge (*'ilm*) is emphasized in Islam as an important activity besides its dissemination. It has been made compulsory (*fardh*) upon its adherents, regardless of gender, to learn and disseminate knowledge. The obligation of seeking out knowledge is binding upon every Muslim by the command of the Qur'an and Sunnah of the Prophet Muhammed (PBUH), who said "Acquisition of knowledge is compulsory upon every Muslim." Fatah Yasin R.F.B. and Jani Mohd. Shah (2013)

The writers on education and Islam should take notice of focusing on Islam rather than on Muslims. An appreciation of the role of human agency could lead to the recognition that while Islam may have ideals, they were continuously formed and reformed in the interaction between the revelatory text and the concrete realities of Muslims; this was and should continue to be an interpretive and ongoing activity. So for studying the Islamic education, the imposed question to be asked is 'what is the Islamic concept of knowledge?' The use of the term "Islamic" as an adjective can become a totalizing notion constructed to describe Muslims and their cultures. Panjwani Farid (2004)

Knowledge in Islam is not merely important, it also occupies a dominant position in its doctrine. It dominated overall aspects of Muslim intellectual, spiritual and social life. It also enables man to grasp the right meaning or the reality of the signs he observes based on Qur'an and Sunnah. Fatah Yasin R.F.B. and Jani Mohd. Shah (2013)

Islam emphasized two types of knowledge, revealed and earthly—i.e., revealed knowledge that comes straight from God and earthly knowledge that is to be discovered by human beings themselves. Islam considers both to be of vital importance and directs its followers, both men and women, to go and seek knowledge. For Muslims, the Qur'an is the perfect word of God, sacred and therefore cannot be changed. It should be memorized from start to finish. Once a person has memorized it, he/she must reflect on these verses and have a detailed understanding of its meaning and interpretation over the lifetime. A person who has mastered it would carry the knowledge of Islam in his/her heart and spread the word to the ones who encounter him/her. According to Islam, seeking earthly knowledge is also important because earthly knowledge compliments the knowledge revealed by God in the Koran and helps Muslims to live productive and good lives in this world. Anzar, Uzma (2003)

Knowledge in Islam and an Islamic approach to education have been domains of contestation and the core of scholarly debates and contentions across the Muslim world. Daun H. and Arjmand R. (2018). The traditional Islamic thought tends to identify the totality of knowledge as religious knowledge. The typology of knowledge in Islam divides the entire human knowledge into two all-embracing categories:

(a) al-ulūm al-aqlīyah (rational/argumentative knowledge).
(b) 'al-ulūm al-naqlīyah (knowledge by transmission).

With this typology, knowledge of various nature fall into one of the categories of the two-fold taxonomy: they either belong to the first type known as *al-'ulūm al-aqlīyah'* (argumentative knowledge); or they are part of the second category labelled as '*al-ulūm al-naqlīyah*' (knowledge by transmission).

Hence, two distinct approaches to knowledge acquisition appear in Islam, each of which is established in the form of various theories of knowledge within the Muslim epistemology. "The first approach is the knowledge as the direct divine illumination, a prophetic approach for which human spiritual development is required. The second approach, however, relies on a philosophical methodology: to understand unknown phenomena through the known ones. While the latter moves from the imagination upward to the theoretical intellect, the prophetic approach takes the reverse path, from the theoretical intellect to the imagination. For this reason, knowledge of philosophy is knowledge of the natures of things themselves, while knowledge of prophecy is knowledge of the natures of things as wrapped up in symbols, the shadows of the imagination. The philosophical approach requires scholastic methodologies to knowledge acquisition and the process of knowledge attainment is gradual. The prophetic knowledge, however, could not be gained in the same philosophical manner". Daun H. and Arjmand R. (2018:6)

This division of knowledge conceptualizes the foundations of the Islamic epistemology and forms the educational arrangements in Islam as well as approached to knowledge acquisition. The approaches to knowledge were utilized extensively not only to explain the notion of knowledge in Islam but also the trend of Islamization of knowledge in a Muslim society. Educational policies and practices, both formal and non-formal, across the Muslim world are informed and inspired by such epistemological models for knowledge acquisition. Daun H. and Arjmand R. (2018) mentioned that according to the approaches to the Islamic education, there are four major approaches to education and knowledge acquisition include:

1. Constructivist Approach to Knowledge which is using rules of logics and *qiyās* (analogical deductive reasoning) aims to attain human knowledge.

2. *Kalāmī* (Theological) Approach to Knowledge which is based on *kalām* (dialectical theology) aims to decipher the divine knowledge as well as mundane one.
3. Philosophical Approach to Knowledge which is inspired and informed by the Neo-Platonist movement and Peripatetic Islamic philosophy in which knowledge is attained through the process of *wham* (estimation) and using the active intelligence to achieve the unknowns through the known premises.
4. Mystical/Theosophical Approach to Knowledge: Knowledge by Presence which argues for the notion of knowledge by presence. The mystical approach rests on the argument on the divine knowledge as the source of all knowledge and intuition as an instrument to achieve it. Daun H. and Arjmand R. (2018:4)

Yet another classification of knowledge under the category of religious sciences, which is not necessarily antithetical to the Muslims' quest for knowledge towards understanding the world around them. Nevertheless, Muslim scholars tend to discard the inclusion of other disciplines of science related to the world, such as medicine, arithmetic, etc., as part of religious sciences, but classed them as techniques. Fatah Yasin R.F.B. and Jani Mohd. Shah (2013) wrote "Modern scholars, such as al-Attas, have divided knowledge into two major categories, religious and rational sciences:

a. *Religious sciences*. This include:

i. The Qur'an and knowledge derived from it such as its recitation, interpretation, *tafsir* and *ta'wil.*
ii. The Sunnah: the life of the holy Prophet, the history and message of the Prophets before him, the Hadith and its authoritative transmission.
iii. The *Sharia'ah:* jurisprudence and law, the principles and practice of Islam.
iv. Theology: God, His essence, attributes and names and acts (*al-tawhid*).
v. Islamic metaphysics (*al-tasawwuf*): psychology, cosmology and ontology; legitimate element of Islamic philosophy including valid cosmological doctrines pertaining to the hierarchy of being.

vi. Linguistic sciences: Arabic, its grammar, lexicography, and literature.

b. Rational, intellectual, and philosophical sciences:

i. Human sciences
ii. Natural sciences
iii. Applied sciences
iv. Technological sciences"

"Islamic epistemology primarily addresses the classic questions about the possibility, nature, and sources of knowledge. Knowledge in Islam is sharply divided into divine and mundane, the latter subordinate to the former. While the divine knowledge is present and is only accessible to the Prophet through revelation, the mundane is acquired by scholastic means. The divine knowledge ultimately is identical with human knowledge while at the same time it is somehow of higher order, both quantitatively and qualitatively". Daun H. and Arjmand R. (2018:5). While the concept of "*ilm*" (knowledge) designates religious as well as mundane knowledge, the predominant trend in traditional Islam was to identify the totality and specify knowledge as religious knowledge. The epistemological principles in Islamic education have informed not only various approaches in the acquisition of knowledge but also institutions of education and learning. The philosophical approach requires scholastic methodologies to knowledge acquisition and the process of knowledge attainment is gradual.

Materializing the Concept and Islamic Education Philosophy

In materializing the concept and philosophy of education in Islam, Fatah Yasin R.F.B. and Jani Mohd. Shah (2013) have suggested "the following strategies to be practiced in the existing educational institutions in Muslim countries, throughout all levels:

1. Education in Islam is not merely of acquiring intellectual knowledge but it is a mean of moulding the nature and character of an individual so that they can collectively represent Islamic values and behave as *khalīfatullāh fī al-ardh* (vicegerent of Allah on the earth).

2. Al-Ghazālī classified both religious and techniques sciences into obligatory (*fardh ʻayn* obligation towards the Self) and meritorious (*fardh kifāyah*—obligation towards Society). While Al-Attas divides knowledge into religious sciences and rational, intellectual, and philosophical sciences. But both agreed that all come from Allah.
3. Establishing an integration between Religious Islamic knowledge and Modern Secular Knowledge by not compartmentalizing Islam as only one subject taught in schools, but Islam is a way of life that applies in all sort of knowledge.
4. The concept of education in Islam must take into consideration of all the dimensions consist of *tarbiyyah, ta'līm* and *ta'dīb*. What does it matter is not the concept, but the practice, methodology and its objectives.
5. *Tarbiyyah* denote the development and training of people in various aspects and to describe the process of upbringing the children as the parents provide them with the physical, educational, moral, and spiritual needs to help them grow and become useful parties in the society.
6. *Ta'līm* is the development of knowledge through the process of teaching and learning (instruction).
7. *Insan adabi* (Perfect Man) is the one who is sincerely conscious of his responsibilities towards the true God; who understands and fulfils his obligations to himself and others in his society with justice, and who constantly strives to improve every aspect of himself towards perfection.
8. Secularism in education has resulted in dualism where an Islamic study is compartmentalized into one independent subject or specialization. As a result, a student of such system will graduate as a professional in either religious knowledge or secular but none will master both. It is a normal phenomenon, that the later will have lack of knowledge of religious matters including *fardh ʻayn* while the former will be illiterate in sciences and modern knowledge.
9. Reformation of Teachers training methodology and evaluation system to ensure that the teachers and educators are well equipped with sufficient knowledge and understanding of the philosophy of Islamic education before educating and teaching the youth.

10. Serious assessment on student's Islamic moral and ethical, in addition of examination and class assessment. For example, student who score high marks in examination is not necessary considered as an excellent student unless he/she is also behaved.
11. The main responsibility for students' education falls on parents who take credit for their probity and bear the burden of their errors, while teachers are only sharing part of this responsibility. An understanding that need to be propagated to the society by the stakeholder". pp.14-5.

Islamic Tradition and Reform in Education

Is Islamic education necessarily traditional education or perhaps it should be understood as education of tradition? Any attempt to answer this question would necessarily involve a close examination of what we understand by the term Islamic tradition. "The notion of Islamic tradition is too broad and abstract to be of much practical use in designing education for any particular society. Hence, distinction must be made between the Islamic tradition and Muslim traditions. One major distinction is that while the Islamic tradition is one, there are as many Muslim traditions as there are Muslim societies". Kazmi Yedullah (2003:283). The Islamic tradition should be seen as the sea that the several Muslim traditions feed, and as Muslim traditions change over time so does the Islamic tradition. The Islamic tradition should be viewed not as a monolithic structure that towers above all Muslim traditions but rather as multifaceted, multicoloured.

According to Tan Charlene (2014), there are three key characteristics of an Islamic tradition:

- First, an Islamic tradition is composed of not just religious beliefs but also political, social and cultural values, beliefs, logics, assumptions and practices that are crucial for the identity formation of its members. An adherence to a tradition entails that members share a common set of core beliefs that both define and is defined by that tradition. The core beliefs include concepts such as 'knowledge', 'modernization', 'rationality, 'critical thinking', 'evidence' and 'autonomy' that are understood and acquired within the context of a specific tradition.

- Secondly, while a community with an effective programme of enculturation is likely to nurture members who are bonded by a set of common beliefs, not every member of an Islamic tradition holds the same beliefs, or holds them to the same degree of commitment. Such variations among members are due to the disparate ways in which they subscribe to their *control beliefs*. Adherence to an Islamic tradition entails those members of a Muslim community hold on to the same set of control beliefs that belongs to their tradition, albeit to different degrees, due to contingent factors such as one's family profile and upbringing, educational background and a myriad of life experiences.
- Thirdly, an Islamic tradition is not static and unchanging. Rather, it is constituted and reconstituted through the ongoing interaction between the present and the past. The discourses in a tradition "relate conceptually to *a past* (when the practice was instituted, and from which the knowledge of its point and proper performance has been transmitted) and *a future* (how the point of that practice can best be secured in the short or long term, or why it should be modified or abandoned), through *a present* (how it is linked to other practices, institutions, and social conditions."

The Origin and Evolution of Islamic Education

"Medieval world is characterized by the dominance of Islam, and Islam owes its origin and rise to the revelation of holy Qur'an to mankind. Obviously, the history of Islamic education began with the copying, understanding and preaching of holy Qur'an. It served as the spring of all Islamic sciences, which originated and developed in course of time. Since Mohammad (P.B.U.H.) was the prophet and transmitter of the divine revelation, the study of his life and actions received equal attention." Afzal Ahmed (2017:25)

"Islamic education owes its origin to the revelation of Qur'an. House of Arqam and later Masjid Nabawi served as the places of education. Within a short span education spread all over the Islamic rule. Its rapid growth can be understood by the fact that before Islam there were only seventeen persons who could read and write but within a short period of Islamic rule every village has *Kuttab* and every mosque came to be a place of learning." Afzal Ahmed (2017)

The first phase of Islamic mosques were used as centres of education. Attention was paid primarily to the teaching of Holy Qur'an, Hadith, and Fiqh. Lessons were imparted verbally and the use of books had not yet taken place. The mosque was the first school in Islam. In the early days of Islam, there was no hierarchy and everyone who could master the content of the Qur'an could lead the prayers and guide the people. The learned people would usually spent most of their time in the mosques debating and polishing their knowledge of the Qur'an and others who could not accord much time to this activity would simply seek their assistance in matters of daily lives. Anzar, Uzma (2003)

After the death of the Prophet, when Muslims faced situations for which no answer could be found in the revealed knowledge of the Qur'an and the Prophet was not there to guide them, the Muslim scholars sought answers in the sayings and practical life of the Prophet. This led to the development of traditions of following the *Sunna,* the knowledge of deeds of the Prophet and *Hadith,* the sayings of the Prophet. The mosque continued to be the centre of learning even after Prophet's death. This mosque based understanding and acquisition of knowledge worked very well for the Muslims of the Arabian Peninsula because the tribal traditions combined with the teachings of the Qur'an were sufficient to govern the lives of people who spoke the same language and had the same cultural background. Anzar, Uzma (2003:2-3)

"However, as Islam expanded to other regions and came into contact with other indigenous traditions and languages, it became necessary to create a cadre of Muslim experts who would develop sophisticated writings and textbooks on *Fiqa* – Islamic jurisprudence, *Sunna* – Prophet's traditions, *Hadith*– Prophet's sayings, and *Tafseer* – the interpretation of the Koran, to cater to the needs of non-Arab Muslim populations. Thus began the tradition of Madrasa, the centre for higher learning, the initial purpose of which was to preserve religious conformity through uniform teachings of Islam for all". Anzar, Uzma (2003:3)

The second phase of educational development began with the ascension of the Omar bin Abdul Aziz. During his rule scattered information relating to Hadith was collected with great vigour and unauthenticated Hadith were weeded out. These were duly compiled and edited and copies were sent to different provincial centres. Arabic syntax was developed for correct recitation and understanding of the Qur'an. In order to free the teachers of the burden of Welihood and encourage students to devote themselves solely to learning, the practice of stipend was introduced. Attention were initiated to widen the horizon of Arab knowledge and wisdom. As a part of this scheme knowledge contained in non-Arabic sources were translated into Arabic, which gave birth to the institution of translation bureau. Other branches of knowledge developed were Kalam, Maghazi, Siyar, history, Arabic literature, grammar, poetry, medicine, logic and Mathematics.

The salient feature of the second phase of education was that mosques still served as centres of education. Although arrangements were also made to set up permanent lecture centres, translation bureau or academies gave a fillip to education. In respect to the methodology, dictation and writing was given importance along with memorization and verbal teaching. Libraries were established and students were given certificates for their ability and performance. Afzal Ahmed (2017)

The third phase is characterized by further progress and maturity of the trends initiated earlier. Mosques continued to serve as educational centres but separate buildings for educational purpose were also constructed with living and fooding arrangements for teachers and students. Study materials were supplied to them. Books were standardized for different curriculum. Specialization of different branches of knowledge was initiated. Eminent teachers and scholars were appointed as teachers on a handsome salary. All this was possible because wealthy persons as well as Muslim philanthropist would donate vast proportion as endowment to these educational institutions. Opening new schools was considered an act of religious piety. Teaching profession commanded great respect and honour. Warriors and administrators with scholastic leanings were often invited to give lectures, some of whom even established their private study circles.

The importance of Islamic culture has evolved in relation to historical circumstances. Western colonization has had a big impact on its social standing. In Arab and Muslim countries emerging from Western European domination, Arab-Islamic culture is no longer the focus of their programmes of study. However, this does not mean that the population's demand for training in the Islamic Sciences has weakened. Their attachment to the first educational system is still seen, although it is difficult to measure. Because it is not well linked to the official political-economic system, the interest attached to it may not be well perceived. As a result, the opportunity cost would be heavy for persons attending this system. Nevertheless, the demand for training in Islamic Sciences is still important, but it is of great demand to be trained for the needs of the work-market as well which requires pursuing modern institutions which teach modern sciences and professional skills. Sall, Mamadou Youry (2016)

Muslims have been reviewing, improving and renewing Islamic education for many centuries. Their reforms of religious educational systems and institutions are underpinned by two distinctive ideas: that the acquisition of knowledge is both a lifelong pursuit and a religious duty for Muslims, and that there must be a correlation between knowledge and action for the welfare of the Muslim community and humanity in general. "Although reform in Islamic education is not a new phenomenon, it reached a turning point during the second half of the nineteenth century amidst European colonization and the concomitant decline of Muslim societies". Tan Charlene and Salleh Hairon (2014:4)

With European colonialism of the Muslim lands, came a new modern system of education that sought to replace the role of Madrasas in any type of development. In the new schools, only those elite were invited to obtain admission that could be used to run the machinery of colonialism. "This resulted in a dichotomy of education system – secular education for the elite and religious education for the poor. The new Western powers also brought the idea of separation of state and religion, which for the Muslim leaders was synonym to heresy. The new system of governance did not require legitimization through religion and this was seen by Islamic scholars as a direct threat to the established code of conduct for the Muslim rulers and their own power. They were not happy with the new changes". Anzar, Uzma (2003:5)

Not only did colonialism challenge the status of Islam in Muslim countries, it also imposed on these countries two major changes that had far-reaching repercussions. The first was the introduction of secular laws that were supported by foreign state apparatuses, modes of administration, law and social institutions. The second major and related change was the introduction of 'modern' Western-type education. Such an education was marked by the promotion of the language of the colonial powers (such as

English, French or Dutch), limited enrolment of a select number of locals at European schools, and dual nature of the colonial school system.

In concert with the promotion of secularism, secular education was introduced where it aimed principally at the development of the rational life of every individual, premised on a form of reality that is restricted to sensual experience, scientific procedure or processes of logic. Hence, the impact of colonialism was that Islamic education was sidelined, relegated to private education and left to the management of Muslim organizations and individuals.

"In response to the onslaught of colonialism and marginalization of Islamic education, Muslims reacted in various ways. Broadly speaking, the Muslims tended towards either being 'traditionalist' or 'reformist', with variations in between, depending on their views (control beliefs) on the place of academic subjects *vis-à-vis* religious subjects in the Islamic education curriculum". Tan Charlene (2014:6) The 'traditionalists' either resisted any attempt to introduce 'modern' academic subjects in the Islamic schools, or allowed limited learning of these subjects with priority given to religious subjects. On the other hand, 'reformists' believed that madrasas should be 'modernized' through the learning of academic subjects within an Islamic framework so that the graduates, whether as future religious leaders or professionals holding secular jobs, could be empowered with the wherewithal to provide answers to modern questions and challenges in a globalized world. Tan Charlene (2014)

The impact of secularism continued after colonialism where Muslim leaders of the newly independent countries – themselves beneficiaries of secular and modern education – sought to reform and modernize their countries along the lines of Western development paradigms. Such an attempt naturally led to uneven developments and different degrees of success across Muslim countries. "Take the examples of Iran and Turkey: while both countries attempted to secularize their states and education systems, the progress in Iran was cut short by the Iranian revolution that reinstalled Islamic influence in education whereas Turkey experienced a gradual restoration of Islam in education after Ataturk's modernizing efforts in the 1920s. But what is common in many post-colonial Muslim countries is the perpetuation of 'educational dualism': two parallel systems of education in operation – Islamic and secular – that uphold mutually exclusive and possibly contradictory educational philosophies and practices". Tan Charlene and Salleh Hairon (2014:6)

A Quest for Reforms in Islamic Education

The reform of Islamic education is a hotly contested issue among Muslim societies since the time of introduction of Islamic reforms, renewal and modernization, in the late nineteenth and early twentieth centuries. Muslims have been polarized in their responses to the idea of reforms in Islamic education. Tan Charlene (2014)

Contributing towards the evolving nature of Islamic traditions is reform in Islamic education. The concept of reform is not new in Islam. The word 'reform' is implied in the terms *tajdid* and *islah* that are found in the Qur'an, *hadiths* and contemporary Islamic literature. Tan Charlene (2014:3) The verb root of this noun [*tajdid*] can be found in a famous *Hadith* of the Prophet Muhammed: 'God will send this [Muslim] community, every hundred years, someone/some people who will renew [*yujaddidu*] its religion.' Tan Charlene (2014:3)

Further, "This is also the meaning of the concept of 'islah' that appears several times in the Qur'an and in some Prophetic tradition (ahadith); it conveys the idea of improving, purifying, reconciling, repairing, and reforming. This is the meaning the prophet Shu'ayb conveys to his people when he says in the Qur'an: 'I do not desire, in opposition to you, to do that which I forbid you to do. I desire nothing but reform [betterment, purification] (al-Islah) as far as I am able. 'It can be understood, then, that the two notions of tajdid and islah convey the same idea of reform and are at the same time complementary since the former primarily (but not exclusively) refers to the relationship to texts, while the latter mainly has to do with reforming the human, spiritual, social, or political context". Tan Charlene (2014:3)

To reform Islamic educational System, the following pertinent questions on reforms in Islamic education may be asked:

- Educational aim: Should Islamic education exist solely or primarily to train Islamic scholars and teachers, or should it have the (added) mission of preparing Muslims to become professionals in the modern world? What should be the

Islamic discourse that underpins the educational aims of Islamic educational institutions? How should Islamic educational institutions and their leaders respond to globalization and modernization?

- Models of Islamic education: Should Islamic educational institutions be state run or privately owned? State-funded or self-funded? Mixed or gender segregated? Specialized or comprehensive? Islam-centric or multicultural?
- Curriculum: What subjects should be included in the curriculum for Islamic educational institutions? How should Islamic education be taught? Should it be taught in an Islamic school where Islamic subjects are given equal or more curriculum time compared to non-Islamic ('secular') subjects, or should it be taught as a stand-alone subject in a secular school? Tan Charlene (2014:8)

Islamic Education System

The need for an Islamic education system is not only a matter of conviction, but also crucial for mankind. No other system can save human beings from destruction and perdition, apparent to anyone with insight into and concern for human welfare. On such a system depends the future well-being of all peoples of the world and this is what Islamic education seeks. Panjwani Farid (2004).

Islamic education system consists of several elements, namely: the basis and objectives of Islamic education, Islamic education curriculum, and methods of Islamic education, educational tools and assessment (evaluation). The purpose of education is the educational component that plays a role affecting other components such as educational materials, educational methods, teaching and learning process, educational attitudes, learners' attitude and evaluation. We can take some components of the Islamic education system that are directly related to the current process of education in Indonesia, including: educational objectives, educational curriculum, approaches and methods of education and evaluation or educational assessment. Yaman, B. and Gultom F. Br. (2017)

Educational Objectives

The aim of education in Islam as stipulated in the First World

Conference on Muslim Education held in Jedda-Mecca (1393 A.H.-1977 A.D.) is to produce a good man. It aims at the balanced growth of the total personality of man through the training of man's spirit, intellect, the rational self, feelings and bodily senses. It caters for the growth in all aspects including spiritual, intellectual, imaginative, physical, scientific, linguistic, both individually and collectively, and incorporate all these aspects in a holistic system of education towards goodness and the attainment of perfection. The ultimate aim lies in the realization of complete submission to Allah as the Creator, on the level of individual, community and humanity at large. Fatah Yasin R.F.B. and Jani Mohd. Shah (2013). Further, the aim of education with the purpose of life that is to achieve happiness by getting close to God. Therefore, the aim of education is to cultivate in man a personality that abides by the teachings of religion, and is hence assured of salvation and happiness in the eternal life of the Hereafter.

Education in Islam is a sort of education which trains the sensibility of an individual, in such a manner that their attitude towards life, their actions, decisions and approach to all kinds of knowledge are governed by the spiritual and deeply felt ethical values of Islam. Fatah Yasin R.F.B. and Jani Mohd. Shah (2013)

The purpose of education serves as the direction to go. With clear objectives, other educational components will always be guided by the objectives, so that the educational process can be measurable and more effective.

The purpose of education is not a fixed and static thing, but it is the whole of one's personality with regard to all aspects of his life, that is, the personality of the person who makes him the "Insan Kamil" with the taqwa pattern. Insan Kamil means human beings who are intimately spiritual and physical that can live normally and normal development because of their taqwa to Allah. For Yaman, Basyir and Gultom Fades Br. (2017:2783), "here are the four goals of Islamic education:

1. The Purpose of Physical Education (al-Ahdaf al-Jismiyah). Prepare yourself as the bearer of the Khalifah on earth through physical skills. Imam Nawawi argues about the "al-qawy" interpretation as strength of faith supported by physical strength (Surat al-Baqarah: 247, al-Anfal: 60)

2. The Purpose of Spiritual Education (al-Ahdaf al-Ruhaniyah). Increasing the spirit of faithfulness to God alone and exercising Islamic morality exemplified by the Prophet Muhammad based on ideal ideals in the Qur'an (Surah Ali Imran: 19). The indication of spiritual education is non-duplicity (Surat al-Baqarah: 10), seeks to purify and purify oneself individually from negative attitudes (Surat al-Baqarah: 126) this is called tazkiyah (purification) and wisdom.
3. The Purpose of Reason Education (al-Ahdaf al-Aqliyah). Intelligence directives to place the truth and its causes by studying the signs of God and discovering the messages of His verses that implicate to the increase of faith to Allah.
4. The Purpose of Social Education (al-Ahdaf al-Ijtimaiyah). The purpose of social education is the formation of a complete personality in the social community. The individual identity here is reflected as "al-nas" living in a pluralistic society."

It is important to note that education in Islam aims to educate human beings with knowledge and positive skills, and to instil in them good ethical conducts approved by the Sharia'ah. Muslim students have to be aware that the acquisition of knowledge is "not merely to satisfy an intellectual curiosity or just for material or worldly gains, but to produce rational and righteous human beings, who are able to meet the spiritual, moral and physical needs of their families, their people and mankind". An ideal personality like this is a product of education whose philosophy is founded on faith in Allah and a commitment to realize God-given moral code well-entrenched in the sacred teaching of Sharia'ah. Fatah Yasin R.F.B. and Jani Mohd. Shah (2013)

Simultaneously, education in Islam is not merely of acquiring intellectual knowledge but it is a mean of moulding the nature and character of individuals so that they can collectively represent Islamic values, behave as vicegerent of Allah on earth, to serve as witnesses to truth and noble conducts. In Islam, the concept of knowledge enjoyed such a central place in society unparalleled in other civilizations. It dominated over all aspects of Muslim intellectual, spiritual and social life. Fatah Yasin R.F.B. and Jani Mohd. Shah (2013)

Curriculum in Islamic Education

Islamic philosophy does not view the life as an end but a means to the endless life, hereafter. But modern philosophies of education consider life in this world as its final goal. Even though the views on educational philosophy varies, there may be some similarities in developing the curricula based on each philosophical outlook and its transactional strategies. The curriculum based on Islamic philosophy must be fit to acquaint the learners with his relations to the Creator and the other creatures around him, his responsibilities, duties and role in the society, his mode of approach to all others etc. All the Islamic philosophers kept these things in mind when they developed their philosophical ideas and curricula and determined its transactional methodology. Abdul Waheedu K. (2003)

"Al-Ghazzali recommended a life-oriented curriculum, which must have provision to estimate the ability of the students. He advocated the primary education for women and recommended home science for them. He insisted to include physical science for children. He stated, philosophy is nothing more than commonsense and regulated thinking, so it cannot give us truth equal to revelation". Abdul Waheedu K. (2003:181)

Ibn-khaldun made a most notable suggestion that the early education is to develop the power of expression by study of language; language learning is nothing but a matter of habit formation. His ideas held wide currency in Europe in those days. Probably, Ibn-khaldun's ideas might have influenced Comenius who also directed to teach language at first in primary classes. He advocated everything in the curriculum that might be pleasurable to the children.

"Ibn Rushd is famous in Europe for his theory of the 'Unity of the Intellect'. He also presented 'two truths theory'; one truth for philosophers, which is philosophy and the other is for masses, it is religion. He tried to harmonize the Qur'an and revelation with philosophy and logic. Ibn Rushd recommended to developing the curriculum comprised his main ideas which influenced the modern education. His main ideas are: allegorical interpretation of the scriptures, the theory of two truths, Pan-psychism, eternity and potentiality of matter and emancipation of women etc. He viewed that man must be free from all oppressions and injustice. The curriculum must be suited to realize this goal. Considering all his contributions, it can be undoubtedly stated that no other Muslim thinker influenced the West than Ibn Rushd". Abdul Waheedu K. (2003:182)

If it is associated with the philosophy and system of Islamic education, of course, the curriculum must be integrated with the teachings of Islam itself. So, it can be concluded that all kinds of science contained in the Qur'an should be taught to learners. These sciences include: the science of religion, history, astronomy, earth sciences, psychology, medical science, agricultural sciences, biology, economics and Arabic language. Thus, the curriculum of Islamic education should reflect the ideality of the Qur'an that does not sort and select all types of disciplines and does not separate the science of religion from the general sciences.

Actually, the Islamic educational system and the curriculum differ according to the stage of education and differ with the passage of time as the schooling system undergone development and upgrading. In the following detailed presentation of the educational system applied in the two main types of educational institutions in the Muslim world, namely: Kuttab and Madrasah. Before studying Kuttab and Madrasah as educational institutions in Islam, let's shed the light on the role of the mosque as a place of education.

The structure of the curriculum and operational procedures of the Madrasas vary from region to region. Most of the Islamic learning takes place in Maktab or Qur'anic schools. The common curriculum in Madrasas, in all regions, is Islamic studies and acquisition of greater understanding of Islamic principles that govern day-to-day lives of the Muslims. Therefore, subjects such as Fiqa – Islamic law, Hadith– Prophet's saying, Sunna— Prophet's traditions, Tafseer – interpretation of the Qur'an, and logic form the crux of Madrasa curriculum. Whereas, most Madrasas in Pakistan teach only religious subjects, many Madrasas, such as the ones in Egypt, Indonesia and Bangladesh, also teach secular subjects. Anzar, Uzma (2003)

Curriculum Transaction

The Muslims used certain methodologies to transact the Islamic curricula. Islamic curricula adopt inimitable and indispensable methodologies mentioned in the Holy Qur'an. In the primary and intermediate stages, the Holy Qur'an is given a place of utmost importance. The memorization of certain amount of Qur'an is to be made compulsory requisite for every pupil. All branches of humanities should be free from any material that conflicts with Islamic faith at all stages of education. Questioning and answering was one of the methods of instruction next to memorization. Abdul Waheedu K. (2003)

Discussions and debates were conducted among learned people as the ways of instruction. Sermons consisted of examples or parables also were accepted in the education circles as the medium to transact knowledge. Many books were translated from Arabic into other languages. And some books from other languages also were translated into Arabic. Certain amount of knowledge was transformed to Arabic and to other languages by these steps. The methods of experimentation and observation were also adopted as a technique of acquiring knowledge.

Small group learning method was adopted by the Muslims. The learning material was distributed in small groups of pupils and they had acquired it in the level of mastery learning. Mastery learning, peer group learning and activity-oriented learning etc. are the learning techniques adopted by the Muslims in the early system of Islamic education. Abdul Waheedu K. (2003)

The success of transacting the curriculum mainly depends on the initiative taken by the teacher in enthusiasing the child towards study for self-confidence, self-reliance and self-realization. The mission of Prophet was to teach the people God's message. Holy Qur'an says, "It is He Who sent amongst the unlettered an apostle from among themselves, to rehearse to them, His signs, to sanctify them and to instruct them in Scripture and Wisdom, although they had been, before, in manifest error."

Islamic education culminates in the union of knowledge with action. The Islamist teacher should possess higher ideals and nobler pattern of behaviour always, especially in the presence of the child and thereby encourages him to imitate and act accordingly. This helps character formation in the child. The teacher should be an expert in his field. The learning items should be presented to the children with their active co-operation and participation with interest. The method of teaching, to a large extent, depends upon the capacity, competence and academic qualification of the teacher. He has to adopt the apt method, in teaching, which is relevant and well-fitted according to the level of children. While transacting the proposed curricula, the teacher has to listen to maintain the interest of the child. He may adopt the method from easy to difficult and known to unknown. "The teachers should not push the pupils beyond their capacity, nor attempt to bring them to a level of knowledge which they cannot absorb." Abdul Waheedu K. (2003)

"As far as curriculum transaction is concerned, Islamic education had from its very inception followed very scientific methods like observation, generalization, discussion, debates, sermons, memorization, lateral thinking, activity orientation, meaningful learning, pragmatic approach etc. It is evident from the abovementioned descriptions that Islamic Philosophy gave vital importance to maintaining relationship between pupils and teachers. It is evident that in the system of education there was constant and regular interaction between teachers and pupils which helped to mould the character of the pupils. It has been established that the educational activities were well planned. The educational institutions and activities connected with them were managed with the co-operation of the community". Abdul Waheedu K. (2003:172-3)

Role of Mosque in Islamic Education

The Central Institution in the Islamic education was the mosque. From the days of Prophet and for quite a few centuries thereafter it was a place not only for saying prayers, but also for taking political decision, place for receiving deputation of persons who would visit the Prophet Muhammed and then Amiru'l Mu'minin on official matters. It was also a place for rendering judicial decisions to resolve conflicts between individuals. "The mosques were the centres of elementary and higher learning in the period of medieval Islam. Institutions for higher learning were also established either along with the mosques or under the control of it". Abdul Waheedu K. (2003:170)

Islam emphasizes education very much. Qur'an and Hadith both are full of such exhortations. The Arabic word 'Ilm' (knowledge) in its various derivations has been used 778 times in Qur'an. The mosque has played a significant role in the development of an independent Muslim educational institution, namely kuttab and madrasah. It was argued that, the process of shaping the independent Islamic educational institutions of kuttab and madrasah was made in three places of education: from Masjid, to the Masjid-khan complex, to the Madrasah. Masjid, hence, is considered the first educational institution in Islam. Also, majlis was the first educational institution which emerged in the mosque as a common practice after the daily prayers, an institution which is extensively in practice across the Muslim world today.

The educational system began with the creation of explanatory circles at mosque schools, which date back to the Prophet Mohammed, who used to give instruction and explanation of his revelations at the mosque. The method of instruction closely resembled that of Aristotle, with the teacher seated in the front surrounded by students, who were arranged in order of importance or longevity of study. Halqha instruction led to the establishment of mosque schools (masjid). It is not unreasonable to envision how the mosques became the centre of instruction, paralleling their role as the centre for worship. These became so popular that at least 3,000 of them existed in the 10th century in Baghdad alone. In addition to the masjid was the palace school (similar to the mosque school except in location) and the bookshop school (also similar to the masjid and the palace school, in addition to becoming central book repositories, i.e., libraries). Hilgendorf Eric (2003)

As these individual learning venues became more popular, it was decided that, in the interest of preserving the sanctity of the mosque worship atmosphere, they should constitute an entity that was removed (in location) from the mosque. Thus, these learning environments became centralized under the concept of the madrasa, which literally means "the place for giving lessons." Mosque schools were required to advance the student through the Qur'an to give a complete understanding of the fundamental issues of value and morality; these institutions were not meant to challenge the student in pursuits of higher analytic thinking. Hilgendorf Eric (2003)

Since the origin of Islam, Halqas (circles of learners sitting around the teacher) have been held in the mosques. Mosques remained the main place for education till the establishment of the Madrasas. Even after the establishment of Madrasas it remained a place for education for a long time. It was customary for the Prophet and then of his companion to answer questions of the devotees and give proper advice regarding good and commendable religious conduct. Out of this very tradition arose the schools of higher learning through Halqas of the learned teachers who attracted students even from far-off places. Similarly, Madrasas and mosques remained interchangeable for a long time throughout Muslim land. Mosques were educational centre for various kinds of knowledge known to the Arabs at that time. Besides literary studies, exegeses, traditions, Jurisprudence, astronomy and medicine were studied too in the mosques. Even after the emergence of the regular Maktabs (also called kuttab) and Madrasas, mosques continued to be used as places of instruction not only in religious matters but also in secular subjects particularly those which developed along with religious Uloom or were intrinsically related to them. Afzal Ahmad (2017:20)

The significance of majlis in teaching religious knowledge and the sunnah within the institution of masjid. The term majlis originally meant the position assumed by the teacher (Shaikh) when teaching after having performed the ritual prayer in the mosque. Most likely majlis is derived from the Islamic tradition of sitting and listening to the lectures after the daily rituals, denoted mostly a gathering in which the religious knowledge was transferred. Later, however, the use of the term extended to cover all types of educational activities and a number of rituals, through a number of extensions added. Daun H. and Arjmand R. (2018:22)

Masjid al-Nabi in Medina, which was established by the Prophet Muhammad, is considered as one of the early Muslim educational institutions, still in use, with the same educational institutions practicing similar pedagogical methods and traditions as in early Islam. "Even at the time that the Prophet was alive, teaching and studying of science and religion was not limited only to Masjid al-Nabi."

Chronologically, Masjid al-Ḥaram in Mecca is older than Masjid al-Nabī of Medina. However, it served solely for religious purposes. It was not until after the conquest of Mecca in the eighth year A.H. (630 C.E.) that it was used as an educational centre. The jurisprudence circles (ḥalaqat al-fiqhiyyah) in Masjid al-Ḥarām has been considered one of the most distinguished circles in the entire Muslim world where, among others, Abullah ibn 'Abbas (d. 687 C.E.) and Muhammad ibn Idris al-Shafi'i (d. 819 C.E.) established and practiced two dominant schools of jurisprudence along with their respective educational traditions. Daun H. and Arjmand R. (2018:23).

The Kuttab or Maktab: the Elementary School

The earliest, informal institutions of learning in the Islamic world were probably children's schools, such arrangements doubtless going back to the pre-Islamic period, which appeared later in all around the Muslim world under a variety of names. "Such institutions are in the West usually known as Qur'anic schools, in Arabic *kuttab*, in Persian *maktab* or *maktabkhaneh. Kuttab* was in a way the continuation of private home schooling which was an established tradition among aristocratic families in Iran and some other countries. The structure of *Kuttab* varied from one context to next, as many local elements integrated into these institutions". Daun H. and Arjmand R. (2018:18)

Kuttab or Maktab comes from the word kataba which means to write. The popular Kuttab in the Prophet Mohammed's period aimed to resolve the illiteracy in the Arab community. Yaman, B. and Gultom F. Br. (2017). "Kuttab is the institution for teaching to read and write preceded the rise of Islam, but on limited scale. It increased very rapidly after the advent of Islam. Early Muslims who could read and write worked mostly as amanuensis to the Prophet and were engaged in teaching for a very long time to come. The Kuttab was mostly in teacher's house and preserved its independence especially in the east". Afzal Ahmad (2017:15)

"The sources have not yielded any direct information concerning the architecture or curricula of early Madrasas (colleges for higher religious studies) and maktabs". Asimov, M.S. & Bosworth, C.E. (2000:33). Mostly, the maktab was attached to the local mosque and was often located in the teacher's house, where he and his wife looked after boys and girls separately. The basic methods of teaching and education in the maktab are methodically and thoroughly described in one of the works of Abu Ali Ibn Sinä (Avicenna, c. 980-1037), in a chapter entitled 'The Role of the Teacher in the Training and Upbringing of Children'.

Though, there were common (public) *Maktabs* which were often catered by middle class families. The classes, which were meant for the reading and memorizing the Qur'an, took place in the neighbouring mosque or home of the teacher where students paid fees cash or in kind, there were some in house private *Kuttab*s or *Maktabs*.

In-house (private) *maktabs* which took place in the homes of wealthy people and were attended by children of the household and other dependents. A room or a separate part of the building was devoted to *Maktab* where children attended daily classes. Daun H. and Arjmand R. (2018)

Afzal Ahmad (2017:16) describes the In-house or in-Palaces Kuttabs: "In early Islam it was the tradition of the affluent and the wealthy people used to send their children in villages and countryside to be brought up and to leant pure, simple and uncorrupt language. After some time, the practice to educate them in their homes started. It was not confined to the royal family only. But those who could afford used to make arrangements for the education of their children at homes. The curriculum was usually drawn up by fathers to suit his child. The student continued to receive higher education in palaces even after the elementary school age. The teachers here were called the Muaddib. The word is from Adab, a concept which includes both moral and intellectual qualities. Therefore, it was applied in this sense to the tutor who was to promote both the qualities. Although the main subjects were the same, some were added or omitted by the instruction of the elders."

Eligibility of Attending Maktabs

Children started to attend school at the age of six or seven. Parents were recommended not to send their children to school before this age. Whereas the informal kuttabs solely taught Qur'an and rarely simple works of literature, formal kuttabs had a rather well-developed curricula divided into theoretical knowledge and practical skills. While the theoretical part had its own teacher, the practical subjects were taught by an instructor from the respective guild. Daun H. and Arjmand R. (2018:19).

Ibn Sinä wrote that children should be sent to a *maktab* school from the age of 6 and be taught primary education until they reach the age of 14. During which time, he wrote, they should be taught the Qur'an, Islamic metaphysics, Arabic, literature, Islamic ethics, and manual skills (which could refer to a variety of practical skills). The programme of education and training proposed by Ibn Sinä involved sending children to school from the age of 6. He believed that when a child reached that age, it was the duty of the parents to look for a good teacher and tutor, who should be wise, devout, perspicacious and knowledgeable about the methods of moral and intellectual schooling. Ibn Sinä attached great importance to the method of study and held that the child ought not to be immediately tied down to books; teaching should be a gradual process. Asimov, M.S. & Bosworth, C.E. (2000:34).

In his curriculum for children between the ages of 6 and 14, Ibn Sinä included study of the Qur'an, metaphysics, language, adab (belles-lettres), ethics and manual skills. Al-Ghazali, however, was strongly opposed to the teaching in school of adab, which he considered more suited to women. He recommended that children be taught the writings of wise men and that they be introduced to the lives of the main figures in the foundation of Islam, the Companions of the Prophet. He also advised schoolteachers and parents to nurture all the good traits that appear at a youthful age in the behaviour and character of children and, if necessary, to praise children in front of other people and reward them with presents. Asimov, M.S. & Bosworth, C.E. (2000:34-5).

Curriculum in Kuttab

"In Kuttab, Qur'an was taught and elementary religious knowledge imparted. The curriculum of Kuttab centred upon the Qur'an as a reading textbook along with being a holy book for educating principles of Islamic faith and behaviour. With reading and writing the students were taught Arabic grammar, stories of the Prophet, particularly Ahadis relating to Mohammad (P.B.U.H.). This was the first educational institution established in Arabia". Afzal Ahmad (2017).

The teaching of Qur'an was combined with instruction on more important religious percepts and usages, the proper response to Wuzu, Azan and the prayer in the mosque. In the Maktab one of the boys would become the imam to familiarize the students with the practice of joint prayers. Stories of the Prophet (P.B.U.H.) and anecdotes from the life of virtuous persons were also taught to them. Writing was included in the elementary course. In addition arithmetic, grammar and elementary literature were also taught in the Maktabs. Everyday before starting a new lesson, the students were asked to read or recite what he had leamt the previous day. This was to implant well the lesson in the students' mind. The teacher in the maktab was called a Muallim or a Faqih on account of his theological training. Afzal Ahmad (2017:21)

As the curriculum of the Kuttab was mainly based upon the Qur'an, it naturally depended for its sustenance upon the teacher who had learnt the Qur'an. The number of Kuttab in the Muslim world increased rapidly until almost every village had at least one. Learning the Qur'an was the core of this elementary course, followed by religious education left to parents. The main subjects taught in children's school was Adab, so much so, that school of children were called Majlis-ul-Adab. This was the general character of curriculum which nevertheless varied from place to place. Afzal Ahmad (2017)

In Kuttabs, teachers were responsible for literacy and numeracy skills and teacher were leading the practices of riding, swimming, shooting arrows, and some other practical skills like etiquettes. The curriculum both in theory and practice varied from place to place, however, ideally it was composed of writing, reading or recitation, rudiments of arithmetic, ḥadith (mostly those in the favour of knowledge and seeking it), qiṣaṣ al-anbiya' (the legends of the prophets), and selections from poetry (those with moral messages). However, not all the subjects were taught in all Kuttabs. Qur'an was used not only as a religious text but also as a main source for the practice of writing. Pupils practiced writing verses of Qur'an on "*alawḥ*" (wooden tablet). As the verses of Qur'an were regarded sacred, every morning, prior to any other activity, a ritual of cleansing took place in the school where pupils had to wipe out the verses of the Qur'an from their "*alwaḥ*" (wooden tablets). Daun H. and Arjmand R. (2018:20).

According to Abu Ali Ibn Sina, the students, in the maktab or Kuttab are taught a set of texts covering the major sciences available in their age. The texts, which are taught constitute the curriculum of the Maktabs, include: "Klmiya-yi safadat" [The Alchemy of Happiness] by al-Ghazali; "TaTim al-mutacallim tarlq al-tacallum" [Teaching the Student the Method of Study] by Burhan al-Din Zarnüji (twelfth century); "Akhlaq-i Nasirl" [Nasirean Ethics] by Nasir al-Din al-Tusi (thirteenth century); "Akhlaq-i-Jalal" [Jalalian Ethics] by Jalal al-Din Dawani (fifteenth century); and in the exhortations of such classical poets. Asimov, M.S. & Bosworth, C.E. (2000:34).

The Madrasas, Higher Education Institutions in Muslim World

The first educational institution in the Muslim world was the mosque built at Medina early in the seventh century by the Prophet Muhammad and his Companions. From then on, mosques were used for teaching purposes, especially for the teaching of law and theology, but as society developed, study circles were held not only in the mosques but also in the palaces, in the streets and even in the market-places. Nevertheless, the mosque remained pre-eminent for the teaching of theology and jurisprudence, where students sat in a circle at the teacher's feet.

Training in religious law could provide a livelihood and was accordingly popular. For instance, one day in 997, the most illustrious teacher of law in Nishapur drew a crowd of over 500 students, and the successor to the celebrated Imam al-Haramayn Abu '1-Macali Juwayni daily attracted classes of over 300. These classes and study groups constituted a kind of 'free university', for the teachers were not subject to any particular restrictions or obligations and students were free to choose among the available classes, discussion groups and study circles.

During the Abbasid period (from 750 to the middle of the thirteenth century) religious education became a branch of learning in its own right, with some teachers specializing in the Qur'an, theology and jurisprudence, while others studied Arabic language, literature and history. The study circles also grew in number and quality during this period, forming the nuclei of what were to become the madrasas, colleges intended for adults who had already received their primary education in private schools or mosques.

In the 10th century, the madrasa emerged as an independent institution distinct from the mosque, although madrasas—at least in the early days—were set up either for a single jurist or to teach the tenets of a particular legal school. Thus was born a new kind of educational institution, destined in future to become a centre of religious and secular learning in the Islamic world and a place where the representatives of the official class were educated in the spirit of Muslim orthodoxy. Asimov, M.S. & Bosworth, C.E. (2000:37-8)

While "*madrasah*" can now refer to any type of school, the term *madrasah* was originally used to refer more specifically to a medieval Islamic centre of learning, mainly teaching Islamic law and theology, usually affiliated with a mosque, and funded by an early charitable trust known as *waqf*.

Madrasah is the Muslim institution of learning par excellence. As such, it was a natural development of two previous institutions: the masjid, in the role of a college of law and its nearby khān as the residence of the law students in attendance. The first institution called madrasah is dated back to the tenth century C.E. The madrasah is in fact the fruit of the efforts to centralize the scattered educational activities under one roof. Unlike the Western education, Islamic education is not based on the credibility of the institution, rather it relies on the teachers' scientific reputation. It is a learner-oriented system of education in which students are recommended and encouraged to wander from one teacher to another, benefiting from informal discussion circles and where parallel sessions of the same subject provide possibility for the students to choose the best teacher and build up their expertise in their own unique way. The system of madrasah centralized all these activities and made the education more institutionalized and accessible. Even after the establishment of madrasah in the Muslim world, the individual and informal approaches to education and teaching — especially in subjects such as medicine and astronomy — have always been prioritized over the institutional policies. Apprenticeship, wrapped in the new Islamic sūfī tradition of the master and the disciple, was practiced extensively in the newly stablished institution of madrasah. Also, interest in foreign subjects such as philosophy found their grounds to grow there.

"Madrasah came to dominate learning in the Islamic Middle East as much as universities do in the contemporary West (Mottahedeh 1985: 89)." Madrasah was something different in the arena of Muslim education: an independent institution which receives various kinds of endowments for funding the education and research following an established curriculum. The founders of madrasahs, often viziers, sultans, wealthy people, and scholars, usually specified two types of financing for madrasah: a budget to cover the running and administrative costs; and scholarships to admit a large number of students (often boarders). Hence, the madrasah set a model with education under the supervision of paid teachers using a fairly uniform curriculum. They became an important part of every Muslim city, just like a mosque or bazaar. Architecturally, "they were constructed similar to fortresses and like fortresses, they were seen and saw themselves as the primary focus of attempts to preserve learning and defend orthodoxy.

By the fifteenth and sixteenth centuries, there were moves towards integration and specialization, and individual madrasas in Samarkand and Herat, under the influence of the scientific circles that had formed there, now acquired a more clearly defined and well-developed structure as centres of scientific education, with inquiries into such sciences as mathematics, astronomy, medicine, philosophy, theology, languages, literature and music. Asimov, M.S. & Bosworth, C.E. (2000:39).

In the second stage of schooling, Madrasah stage of Islamic education, which Ibn Sinä called the period of specialization, pupils should, in his view, begin to acquire manual skills, irrespective of their social status. He advised teachers and tutors to show the utmost attention and prudence in this transitional stage, making allowances both for the age of their pupils and for their emotional development, since children differ naturally from one another. For instance, some pupils have a flair for reading, others for manual skills, yet others for literature, while some are destined to be preachers; and pupils are drawn to these subjects according to their interests. 'And moving away from the multifarious domain of language', Ibn Sinä wrote, 'one observes that some choose medicine, others geometry; and thus various groups of people specialize in professions that are closest to their hearts.' Ibn Sinä's own preference was for the teaching of crafts, rather than the more risky trade and commerce, since 'the master of a craft, no matter what the circumstances, will always find a use for his skills'. The teaching of such crafts should begin immediately after completion of the study of the Qur'an and basic Arabic grammar. He advised parents not to be over-protective of their children and not to smother them with attention while they were being trained in a craft; rather, they should be given encouragement, and an interest should be taken in the final result of their efforts. Asimov, M.S. & Bosworth, C.E. (2000:35).

Ibn Sinä refers to the educational stage of *Madrasah* schooling system as a period of specialisation when pupils should begin to acquire manual skills, regardless of their social status. He writes that children after the age of 14 should be allowed to choose and specialize in subjects they have an interest in, whether it was reading, manual skills, literature, preaching, medicine, geometry, trade and commerce, craftsmanship, or any other subject or profession they would be interested in pursuing for a future career. He wrote that this was a transitional stage and that there needs to be flexibility regarding the age in which pupils graduate, as the student's emotional development and chosen subjects need to be taken into account. Asimov, M.S. & Bosworth, C.E. (2000).

The Mongol invasion dealt a temporary blow to learning, severing links between creative intellectuals and for a time disrupting the continuity of culture, but after the successful monetary reform introduced by the first Mongols, Mongke Khan and his minister Mascud Beg, economic life soon revived in the cities of Iran and Transoxania. These same rulers encouraged the exact sciences, which, as noted by Bartol'd, they perceived to be of practical use. In this cultural renaissance, particular preference was given to the organizational role of the madrasa as the promoter of literary and scientific thought. Under Mascüd Beg twin madrasas were built in Bukhara, in each of which, according to al-Juwayni, 1,000 students could study. However, during the civil wars of the 1270s, when Bukhara was laid waste for seven years, the madrasas and their libraries were burnt down. Asimov, M.S. & Bosworth, C.E. (2000:38-9)

Under the leadership of al-Tusi, over 100 scientists worked and wrote there, and astronomical observations were carried out there for a period of over 15 years. Attached to the observatory was a madrasa, and lectures there were closely connected to the activities of the observatory. Its teaching covered philosophy, medicine, theology and handasa (technology). Asimov, M.S. & Bosworth, C.E. (2000:39)

Under the Mongols, and later under the Timurids, there was a growing tendency to build at major urban sites architectural ensembles that often included a mosque, a madrasa, a mausoleum and public garmabs (baths), and we have valuable accounts of the construction of madrasas undertaken by Mongol rulers and members of their families in Shiraz, Isfahan, Tabriz, Kirman, Gurganj and other cities in Iran and Central Asia. One of the most important buildings of the late fourteenth century in Samarkand was the Khanum madrasa opposite the famous great mosque of Timur, built in honour of his mother and his wife, Saräy-i Mulk Khänum. Asimov, M.S. & Bosworth, C.E. (2000:40)

Curriculum in Madrasah

The contents of the curriculum, the process of its transaction and evaluation etc. should also be in agreement with the nature of Islamic philosophy. However a man of integrated personality is expected to come out as a product on completion of a course of study under the Islamic curriculum. Abdul Waheedu K. (2003)

The curriculum of any society will reflect its concepts of issues, the ideology and culture it inherits, the goals which it intends to achieve etc. Islamic curriculum familiarizes the individual with his relation to his fellow beings and other creatures, his responsibilities in life, duties and role in the society, his social relation and his relationship with the universe as a whole.

Islamic Education distinguishes clearly between two types of curricula:

(i) Obligatory knowledge which must be studied by everyone. It includes the religious sciences and related disciplines such as linguistics and literature;

(ii) Optional knowledge, which are to be learned according to the interest and capacities of the pupil. They are in turn divided into: (a) revealed sciences, and (b) non-revealed sciences. Abdul Waheedu K. (2003)

The bases of Islamic curriculum are mainly Qur'an and Sunnah. So, it is the prime duty of the curriculum setters not to include any element which may adversely affect the Qur'anic principles. However, a man of integrated personality is expected to come out as a product on completion of the Islamic curriculum.

The Islamic curriculum is ideologically oriented; hence the nature and contents of it and the syllabi will be of the same nature. Islamic education is a life-long process. So, possibility of continuity should be ensured in all stages of education. Qur'anic concept of man is that he is, dignified honourable human being, the vicegerent of God on earth. Accordingly, the curriculum should be framed including the relevant and appropriate topics for preparing the man to undergo a stream of education that will prepare him to perform effectively the duties entrusted upon him. Abdul Waheedu K. (2003)

During its formative period, the term madrasah referred to a higher education institution, whose curriculum initially included only the "religious sciences", whilst philosophy and the secular sciences were often excluded. The curriculum slowly began to diversify, with many later madaris teaching both the religious and the "secular sciences", such as logic, mathematics and philosophy. Some madaris further extended their curriculum to history, politics, ethics, music, metaphysics, medicine, astronomy and chemistry. The curriculum of a madrasah was usually set by its founder, but most generally taught both the religious sciences and the physical sciences.

The first attempt to establish a uniform curriculum in madrasah in the 11th century was not due to the educational needs or pedagogical aims. Uniform curriculum in madrasah was put into practice by Niẓām al-Mulk who is also credited as the innovator of the madrasah system. As Niẓāmīyyah (series of madrasahs founded by Niẓām al-Mulk) were founded to strengthen the Shāfi'ī school of thought, the uniform curriculum was a means to guarantee that the madrasah stays within Shāfi'ī guidelines, regardless of geographical and demographic differences.

The curricula of madrasahs vary not only according to the stipulations of the founders but also according to the preferences of the teachers and the wishes of the directors of madrasahs. The madrasah has always been regarded as the institution for Islamic sciences. Thus, it is expected to provide the basic education in fiqh (religious law, Islamic jurisprudence). Students are expected to be acquainted with the arguments using Qur'ān, ḥadī th (sunnah) and sīrah. Over the course of time, other subjects – some foreign sciences – were introduced to the madrasah curricula.

Like people and races in different parts of the world who enjoyed poetry and heroic songs, pre-Islamic Arabs also had a passion for poetry and ballads. These were, however, largely oral, for literacy existed only among selected few. It was amidst such a socio-intellectual background that the holy Qur'an, which claims to be unique book of all times, was revealed and hence, it was said that it is the first written book in the history of Arabs. It is however, to be noted in its composition the Arabs had nothing to do, they simply served as copyist of the message of God.

The Madrasah System

The education in the early centuries of Islam was being carried out in 'madaris'. These type of schools were connected with a major mosque. The students were accommodated with boarding and lodging facilities. They were not restricted to finish their studies within a particular period of time as modem universities do. No specific degrees were conferred upon them. Most of the Islamic intellectual sciences today are performed outside formal institution. Very often a library was attached along with the madrasah. Abdul Waheedu K. (2003)

According to Islam, education is a powerful instrument for bringing about social change and to put an end to ignorance and superstitions. A teacher is held in high esteem in the Islamic society, even though he may not be wealthy.

Muslims have contributed their mite towards the establishment of Maktabs and Madrasas and provided assistance to students in the form of stipend, books, food and the like. No formal educational institutions were found during the early days of Islam. Classes were held in thc compounds of mosques, in cells and dormitories attached to the residence of the 'Ulema'. The expenses of the madrasas were met from the revenue earned from large estate given as endowments. Certain madrasas had libraries and hospitals attached to it. Abdul Waheedu K. (2003)

History of Islam has proved that Islamic Educational Institutions had their own curriculum and the philosophy of curriculum centred round the Islamic epistemology and axiology which were based on Qur'an and Hadith. It is stated that the mosque was the central institution in the system of Islamic education and Madrasas were attached to it. The facilities for students staying in the educational institutions were made which was later adopted by the system of modern education.

"Based on these historical facts one can come to the conclusion that there was healthy teacher-pupil interaction which resulted in the increase in knowledge of the students and their character formation. Besides, the new system of arrangements made for the studies, and stay of the students make it clear that there was a system of management which was often supported by the rulers of the region as well as the community as a whole. The system of educational management was carried out in the interest of the society based on the principles of Islam". Abdul Waheedu K. (2003:173)

The Evolution in the Educational System of Madrasah

The Madrasah initially was a very simple institution teaching reading and writing. It has been under a palm tree, in a tent or in a private house; yet it was a Madrasa. The courtyard of mosques and the open halls running along the walls of the mosques were also used for the purpose of education as a Madrasah. However, there is a significant difference between the present day Islamic system education which got influenced by the Western education system and the old Islamic system of education.

Islamic education has undergone several changes from the day of its beginning. At the beginning only Qur'an and Hadis and Fiqh was taught. Gradually other branches of knowledge were added to it. All the branches of secular and religious knowledge were taught. Frequent changes were introduced to meet the challenges of the time. But after the introduction of Dars-e-Nizami by Mullah Nizamuddin, the madrasas could not keep pace with the changing times. They clung to the outdated syllabus of the Dars-e-Nizami in its degenerated form. That is why most of the madrasas graduates are unable to take part in the process of national development. Afzal Ahmed (2017)

From the earliest years of their history, Muslims witnessed juxtaposition of their faith and worldly power. Within a hundred years after the death of the Prophet Muhammad, Muslims were ruling over a vast empire. The Qur'anic assurance that "they were the best community" (The Qur'an, 3:110) was nourished and confirmed by this situation, which continued for another thousand years or so. Panjwani Farid (2004). With the territorial expansion of Islam under the pious caliphate new political centres emerged such as Kufa, Basra, Palestine and Damascus. This necessitated the appointment of permanent teachers to these far-flung areas and opening of maktabs. The companions of the Prophet Muhammed were held in great esteem and their lectures and sermons were heard with great eagerness and devotion. The expansion of Islamic empire brought manifold problems because different races of men were brought within the fold of Islam who hitherto held different faiths and followed different polity. Accordingly to meet the requirements Islamic jurisprudence or Fiqh was developed. Afzal Ahmed (2017:26)

Nowadays a Madrasah or a school constitutes a great building, a group of specialist professionals, a series of lectures for certain limited hours. The universities or colleges in the present time can be established only in cities, but old personified Madrasahs of that time could be established in every village, town or hut. In the old terminology, a Madrasah was in the name of a particular person where a great number of people flock towards him and surround him and whatever he would speak day and night, it would be his educational lectures; his manners, postures, gestures, his dress etc. all would be his silent educational lectures.

REFERENCES

Abdul Waheedu K. (2003). Influence of Islamic Philosophy on the Theory and Practice of Education. Ph. D. thesis in Education. University of Calicut, India.

Afzal Ahmad (2017). A Study of Madrasa Education in modern Perspective of Azamgarh and Jaunpur Districts. Ph. D. thesis in Education. Veer Bahadur Singh Purvanchal University, Jaunpur (U.P.) India.

Anwaruddin Sardar M. (2012). Islamic Education and Modernity: An Uneasy Alliance? *The Independent* (A national newspaper in Bangladesh). October 1, 2012.

Asimov, M.S. & Bosworth, C.E. (1998). *History of Civilizations of Central Asia, Vol. 4: The Age of Achievement A.D. 750 to the end of the fifteenth century, Part One: The Historical, Social and Economic Setting.* Paris: UNESCO Publication.

Asimov, M.S. & Bosworth, C.E. (2000). *History of Civilizations of Central Asia, Vol. 4:* The Age of Achievement A.D. 750 to the end of the fifteenth century, Part Two: The achievements. Paris: UNESCO Publication.

Breen Damian (2018). *Muslim Schools, Communities and Critical Race Theory: Faith Schooling in an Islamophobic Britain*? London: Palgrave Macmillan.

Daun Holger and Arjmand Reza (2018). (Eds.) *Handbook of Islamic Education*. Cham, Switzerland: Springer.

Etheredge Laura S. (2010). *Islamic history*. New York: Britannica Educational Publishing.

Fatah Yasin R.F.B. and Jani Mohd. Shah (2013). *"Islamic Education: The Philosophy, Aim, and Main Features". International Journal of Education and Research.* October 2013, Vol. 1 (10), pp. 1-18.

Hilgendorf Eric (2003). "Islamic Education: History and Tendency." *Peabody Journal of Education*, 78(2) : 63-75.

Jimba, Moshood Mahmood M. (2016). *Al-Azhar University's Role in Educating Nigerians: A Case Study of the Ilorin Al-Azhar Institute*. In *Lo, Mbaye and Haron, Muhammed (2016) (Eds.) Muslim Institutions of Higher Education in Postcolonial Africa*. Basingstoke, Hampshire, U.K.: Palgrave Macmillan.

Kazmi Yedullah (2003). "Islamic Education: Traditional Education or Education of Tradition?" *Islamic Studies* 42:2 (2003) pp. 259-288

Noaparast, Bagheri Khosrow (2001). *Islamic Education*. Ph D. thesis, N.S.W. University. Australia.

Panjwani Farid (2004). "The 'Islamic' in Islamic Education: Assessing the Discourse." *Current Issues in Comparative Education*, Vol. 7(1). pp. 19-29.

Sall, Mamadou Youry (2016). *Scientific Profiles and Potential of Al-Azhar's African Graduates: A Statistical Analysis*. In Lo, Mbaye and Haron, Muhammed (2016) (Eds.) *Muslim Institutions of Higher Education in Postcolonial Africa*. Basingstoke, Hampshire, U.K.: Palgrave Macmillan.

Tan Charlene (2014). (Ed) *Reforms in Islamic Education*. London: Bloomsbury Academic.

Tan Charlene and Salleh Hairon (2014). *Curriculum and Pedagogy of Islamic Education*. In Tan Charlene (2014) (Ed) *Reforms in Islamic Education*. London: Bloomsbury Academic.

Tan, Charlene (2014). *Reforms in Islamic Education: International Perspectives*. London: Bloomsbury Academic.

Anzar, Uzma (2003). *Islamic Education: A Brief History of Madrassas with Comments on Curricula and Current Pedagogical Practices*. https://www.researchgate.net/publication/264868678_Islamic_Education_A_Brief_History_of_Madrassas_With_Comments_on_Curricula_and_Current_Pedagogical_Practices.

Yaman, Basyir and Gultom Fades Br. (2017). "Islamic Education System: Implementation of Curriculum Kuttab Al-Fatih Semarang." *International Journal of Educational and Pedagogical Sciences*, 11(12) 2017, pp. 2783-9.

6
Islamic Education: Need to Reform Curriculum

Anjum Ahmed

INITIATIVE TAKEN TO REFORM ISLAMIC CURRICULUM

Introduction to Curriculum

In Latin curriculum was a racing chariot; ***'currere'*** was ***'to run'***. Ever since the term curriculum was added to educators' vocabularies, it has seemed to convey many things to many people. To some, curriculum has denoted a specific course, while to others it has meant the entire educational environment. Whereas perceptions of the term may vary, it must be recognized that curriculum encompasses more than a simple definition. Curriculum is a key element in the educational process; its scope is extremely broad, and it touches virtually everyone who is involved with teaching and learning.

Before defining curriculum development, it is imperative to know the importance of curriculum. A curriculum is considered as the "heart" of any learning institution which means that schools or universities cannot exist without a curriculum. With its importance in formal education, the curriculum has become a dynamic process due to the changes that occur in our society. Therefore, in its broadest sense, curriculum refers to the "total learning experiences of individuals not only in school but society as well" (Bilbao *et al.*, 2008).

Good curriculum plays an important role in forging life-long learning competencies, as well as social attitudes and skills, such as tolerance and respect, constructive management of diversity, promotion and respect of Human Rights, peaceful conflict management and transformation, gender equality, justice and inclusiveness. At the same time, curriculum contributes to the development of thinking and creative skills and the acquisition of relevant knowledge that learners need to apply in the context of their studies, careers and daily life. Curriculum is also increasingly called upon to support the learner's personal development by contributing to enhancing their self-respect and confidence, motivation and aspirations.

Curriculum can be envisaged from different perspectives. What societies envisage as important teaching and learning constitutes the "***intended***" curriculum. Since it is usually presented in official documents, it may be also called the "***written***" and/or "***official***" curriculum. However, at classroom level this intended curriculum may be altered through a range of complex classroom interactions, and what is actually delivered can be considered the "***implemented***" curriculum. What learners really learn (i.e. what can be assessed and can be demonstrated as learning outcomes/learner competencies) constitutes the "***achieved***" or "***learned***" curriculum. In addition, curriculum theory points to a "***hidden***" curriculum (i.e. the unintended development of personal values and beliefs of learners, teachers and communities; unexpected impact of a curriculum; unforeseen aspects of a learning process). Those who develop the intended curriculum should have all these different dimensions of the curriculum in view. While the "written" curriculum does not exhaust the meaning of curriculum, it is important because it represents the vision of the society. The "written" curriculum should therefore be expressed in comprehensive and user-friendly documents, such as curriculum frameworks; subjects syllabi, and in relevant and helpful learning materials, such as textbooks; teacher guides; assessment guides.

Perhaps one of the earliest forms of systematic curriculum building in career and technical education may be attributed to Victor Della Vos, Director of the Imperial Technical School of Moscow. At the Philadelphia Centennial Exposition of 1876, Della Vos demonstrated a new approach to teaching the mechanical arts that "became a catalyst for career and technical education in the United States" (Lannie, 1971). Rather than leaning through conscious imitation, the Russian system utilized shops where formal instruction in the mechanical arts could be provided. This system attempted to teach mechanical arts fundamentals: (a) in the least possible time; (b) in such a way as to make possible the giving of adequate instruction to a large number of students at one time; (c) by a method that would give to the study of practical shop work the character of a sound, systematically acquirement of knowledge; and (d) so as to enable the teacher to determine the progress of each student at any time. (Bennett, 1937)

Definition of Curriculum Development

Curriculum Development is defined as planned, a purposeful, progressive, and systematic process to create positive improvements in the educational system. Every time there are changes or developments happening around the world, the school curricula are affected. There is a need to update them to address the society's needs.

In today's knowledge economy, curriculum development plays a vital role in improving the economy of a country. It also provides answers or solutions to the world's pressing conditions and problems, such as environment, politics, socio-economics, and other issues of poverty, climate change, and sustainable development.

Kerr defines curriculum as, "All the learning which is planned and guided by the school, whether it is carried on in groups or individually, inside or outside the school." (Kelly 1999). This gives us some basis to move on – and for the moment all we need to do is highlight two of the key features:

Learning is planned and guided. We have to specify in advance what we are seeking to achieve and how we are to go about it.

The definition refers to schooling. We should recognize that our current appreciation of curriculum theory and practice emerged in the school and in relation to other schooling ideas such as subject and lesson. There are four ways of approaching curriculum theory and practice:

1. Curriculum as a body of knowledge to be **transmitted**.
2. Curriculum as an attempt to achieve certain ends in students – **product**.
3. Curriculum as **process**.
4. Curriculum as **praxis**.

It is helpful to consider these ways of approaching curriculum theory and practice in the light of Aristotle's influential categorization of knowledge into three disciplines: the theoretical, the productive and the practical.

In order to clarify this concept of curriculum, it is vital to examine how it may be distinguished from the concept of instruction. Whereas curriculum constitutes a broad range of student experiences in the school setting, instruction focuses on the delivery of those experiences. More specifically, instruction may be perceived as the planned interaction between instructors and students that (hopefully) results in desirable learning. Sometimes, serious questions may be raised as to what exactly constitutes curriculum and what constitutes instruction. Some educators feel that any curriculum includes instruction; others contend that sound instruction includes a sound curriculum.

A brief description of curriculum development and instructional development should aid in clarifying these apparent differences of opinion. Curriculum development focuses primarily on content and areas related to it. It encompasses the macro or broadly based activities that impact on a wide range of programmes, courses, and student experiences. In fact, the curriculum should define the institution's mission and goals. Curriculum activities are typically conducted prior to and at a higher level than instructional development. In contrast, instructional development is more of a micro activity that builds on curriculum development through planning for and preparation of specific learning experiences within courses.

Islamic Education and its Curriculum

Islamic Education: It is education in the Islamic spirit which is universal and relevant to all mankind which has no segregation between "religious" and "secular" knowledge. It aims at developing the entire human aspects physically, intellectually and spiritually as well as to educate and to create awareness about his nature as a man and his roles as the servant of God and His vicegerent on this earth.

A serious question arises on how to resolve the issue of dualism or bifurcation in Muslim education system nowadays. This issue is seriously debated among Muslim scholars who have continuously attempted to revive the excellence of the Ummah. ***Ummah*** (Arabic:

امة) is an Arabic word meaning "community". These committed scholars have gathered in the First World Conference on Muslim Education in 1977. They diagnosed that the malaise of Muslim Ummah is through the process of secularizing Muslim children intellectually, mentally and emotionally due to the impact of colonialism in most Muslim countries. Many scholars unfold the chaotic situation occurring in the Muslim Ummah at present, that is, the emergence of two contradictory types of people; people who are too busy with worldly activities, while the other people who are concerned with hereafter matters which create dichotomy in the society.

Ismail Raji Al-Faruqi asserts that the core of the malaise of the Ummah is undoubtedly, its intellectual and methodological decline. The educational system is the breeding ground of the disease. He argues that the present state of education in the Muslim World is at its worst because of its bifurcating curriculum that comprises opposing components, one "Islamic" and one "modern". Lack of clear and specific vision leads to the insoluble problem of low standards in the Muslim World institutions.

In another study, Shahed Ali perceives that a crucial problem faced by Muslims, particularly in education, which arises from its contact with Western philosophy and attitude during imperialism and colonialism. Although Muslim countries have now gained independence they seem to have no choice except to imitate Western styles and also to adopt Western philosophies in order to gain rapid prosperity and material achievement. These Western materialistic and Nihilistic-totalitarian philosophies totally destroy Muslims identities. Fortunately, there are some present Muslims who think about their future as a distinct community and people, having deep roots in their own philosophy. Freda Shamma also exposes that the Western or secular education and its underlying values, which have been integrated into Muslims life, have destroyed the 'Islamic social system'. This phenomena was also studied by another Muslim writer, Tueybaha Sala-ud-Din who believes that the Western education is transplanting its values through the art of 'integration'. In this process of integration, gradually the Muslim children will neglect Islamic values and identity in order to be integrated into the Western system and therefore, make a compromise with Islamic doctrine and ideology. Undoubtedly, the ultimate aim of Western or secular education is to produce secular individuals who will assimilate secular values; and in the future would able to develop secular society.

Another prominent Muslim scholar, Fazlur Rahman comments on the negative Muslims, attitude to knowledge and negligence of AlQur'an in the later medieval centuries that 'perceives both higher knowledge and faith are mutually dysfunctional'. As a result, knowledge becomes 'purely secular' and disintegrates into two different types namely 'religious' and 'secular' sciences. Therefore, he suggests the reformation of traditional education and its integration with the modern knowledge.

Identification of the need of Integrated Islamic Curriculum as an Ummatic Solution, it can be noted that the process of 'integration' in the educational system provides a fertile ground because the period of schooling is very long. Normally, children would spend 2 years for pre-schooling, 6 years for primary and another 4 to 6 years for secondary education, in addition 3 to 4 years at the tertiary level. Starting from earliest age of 3 to 4 years at the nursery, the Muslim children are already exposed to numerous elements of schooling and its surroundings, and continuously absorb the underlying values in various approaches of integration. Thus, the effect of values in education within the social system is inevitable. The environment should also be taken into consideration in order to achieve the success of the educational process of integrating values. In this case, Muslims are obliged to focus on the nature of knowledge and its values that should be transplanted or integrated in their children's minds, souls and attitudes. Here, the significance of the concept of 'integration' is obvious in the educational system and its curriculum.

Ghazali Basri, also supports the idea of integration and he claims that an integrated knowledge is essential in developing every aspect of human potentials and producing a well-balanced being. For him, the development of mental, physical, emotional, ethical and aesthetical aspects cannot be enhanced without the process of integration in the educational system. He strongly believes that Islam perceives all types of knowledge are complementary meaning that 'empirical, sensory and intellectual knowledge' have never been divorced from Divine knowledge. Therefore, disintegration of knowledge from its 'unitary form' will lead to 'compartmentalization of knowledge' that is contradictory to Islamic tradition.

Our brief review indicates that most Muslim educators, academicians and scholars have reached a conclusion that there is a need to provide a truly Islamic system of education that can benefit all Muslims. This system should be able to create Ummatic consciousness towards social Islamic solidarity by instilling the sense of brotherhood instead of selfishness amongst Muslims regardless races, countries, nations and origins. This solidarity is essential for the Ummah as a means to achieve happiness, prosperity and peace. It is mentioned explicitly in the Qur'an and the Hadith. Allah says "The believers are but brothers." (49:10) and "The Believers, men and women, are protectors, one of another." (9:71). Prophet Muhammad gave analogy: "A believer to another believer is like a building whose different parts enforce each other."

Freda Shamma has suggested that a good solution to this phenomenon is a 'marriage between the traditional and modern Westernized school.' She claims that this solution 'acts as a precursor to the modern Islamic schools'. This new type of Islamic educational institution attempts to integrate harmoniously both kinds of education i.e. Islamic and modern. Consequently, Islamic private schools that provide an alternative that is a combination of both modern secular and Islamic religious curricula were established. In these modern private Islamic schools, the individuals involved were able to make decisions and policies in curriculum planning in accordance with their common needs and problems. Their aspiration is producing a well-balanced individual.

Snapshot of Islamic Curriculum

It is important to know that in India, Islamic education is given in madrasah and non-madrasah (Regular school). To clarify the meaning and concept of madrasah, it is seen that the word "madrasah" is Arabic which translates to 'school'. It is derived from the root word 'dars', which connotes a learning process carried through drill lesson. Also derived from the same root are: (1) mudarres, meaning a male teacher, while mudarresah is a female teacher; and (2) derrasah, meaning studying or studied subject. (Ismael, 1995). In the Islamic religion, madrasas are important centres for learning not only about Islam, but about secular subjects as well. In madrasahs Islamic theology and law, Arabic grammar and literature, mathematics, logic, and, in some cases, natural science is taught. Today, madrasahs balance religious education with the study of secular subjects. However, the curriculum in madrasahs depends on the location of the school. For example, madrasahs in Western countries are more likely to promote math and other subjects than their non-Western counterparts. In Western countries, madrasahs serve as a place for Muslims to come together and bond. In non-Western countries, madrasahs are the cornerstone for education, and aid impoverished families seeking an education, food and housing for their children. In Indian subcontinent Madrasah is of two types: (1) where only religious i.e. Islamic knowledge is provided with the help of the Qur'an and the Hadith (saying and doing of Prophet Mohammad, PBUH) and (2) where the modern and religious education is provided simultaneously. Modern education consists of knowledge of science, mathematics, technology and English etc. Madrasah are further classified as residential and non-residential, private (run by an individual or an organization or society) and public (recognized by the government like madrasah board of state government or the wakf board).

In the state of Uttar Pradesh, madrasah are recognized by UP Board of Madrasa Education, Lucknow (UPBME) (under the Department of Minorities Welfare & Wakf, Government of UP). The Madrasah Board is very popular in UP state. Madrasah Board conduct the Munshi, Maulvi, Alim, Fazil, Kamil every year. In some madrasah contemporary education is provided to cope with the modern technological and scientific educational processes. Students are also trained in co-curricular activities, games and sports. They are supposed to be good debaters, leaders, artisans and social being.

The Nature of the Curriculum of Islamic Education

Topics covered in Qur'an and Islamic education in the primary grades include basic Muslim beliefs (the pillars of Islam, the statements of faith, revelation [*wahi*], afterlife, the characters of God, belief in the angels of God), basic rituals (prayers, fasting, ablution, alms [*zakat*]), and general Muslim etiquette (the ethics of walking and eating, dealing with neighbours, parents, relatives, animals, and birds). In high school, students are introduced to more advanced topics, including: Islamic punishments (*hudud*) for apostasy, theft, adultery, and drinking, corporal punishments

(*ta'zir*), political system in Islam, suicide, the scientific miracles of the Qur'an, the purposes of *shari'a,* contracts, jihad, and peace.
The following topics are suggested to be included in the Islamic curriculum:

- Concept of Monotheism
- Basic Pillars of Islam
- Patience of the Prophet
- Seerah of Prophet
- Moral lessons from the stories of different prophets of Islam
- Isra' and Mi'raj (The night journeys Muslims believe the Prophet undertook to Jerusalem and paradise)
- Prophet's immigration to Medina
- Loving the Prophet and following his footsteps
- Greatest polytheism
- Belief in angels
- Belief in the heavenly books
- Need to protect our natural resources
- Loving good for others
- Importance of patience, tolerance and controlling anger
- The attributes of a true Muslim
- Importance of seeking knowledge
- Impurities and their kinds
- Conditions for ablution
- Enjoining the lawful earthly goods
- Being contented and importance of gratitude

For secondary and higher secondary level, topics should be based on the life skills, critical thinking and problem solving skills:

- The impact of faith on the life of an individual
- The position of women in Islam
- The Mothers of the Faithful
- Marriage and Parenting
- Killing oneself (suicide)
- The punishment for apostasy
- Those who remained behind in the battles
- The impact of faith on the life of society
- Trust in God

- Resolving conflict effectively
- Negotiation skills
- Bantering and its etiquette
- The punishment for theft, unlawful warfare, and adultery
- Arab delegations to the Prophet
- Belief in the afterlife
- Martyrdom for the cause of God
- Islamic unity
- Felonies and corporal punishments in Islam
- The Prophet's farewell lecture
- Importance of Prayers
- Political system in Islam
- Earning livelihood in Islam
- Time Management
- Islam and Social Media
- Islam and Science

Islamic education textbooks should represent both the Sunni and Shiites versions. There are also four Sunni schools of thought. The textbooks should emphasis ***"true" Muslim community***, and not amplify the difference between the groups and compartmentalize the true essence of Islam. The differences should be respected and not become the subject of ridicule or objection. Followers of all the groups are all followers of the singular, true Islam.

Islamic education textbooks do not place a heavy emphasis on the ***history of Islam*** and how the Islamic movement spread from the Arabic peninsular. Similarities between Christianity, Judaism and Islam should be highlighted.

Raising God-conscious, moral, successful children with a sense of civic responsibility in today's world is not easy. It is also not impossible. Effective parenting is the key. Dr. Hisham has written a new book on ***Islamic parenting*** a very essential topic discussed in psychology and very pertinent to Islam. He asserts that the recipe for a healthy family and community is one and the same as the recipe for a peaceful Islamic society. With the inspiration of verses such as 75 of the chapter Al-Furqan, Dr. Hisham laid out the wish list of a happy family that aims to raise leaders of the pious. He emphasized the need to address physical and mental health as interdependent, integral factors. He also underlined the importance of a parent not just as an example of achievement and success, but also of honesty and humility: this, he argued, would be the best way attract your children's respect. Dr. Imad-ad-Din Ahmad, who reflected on his chaplaincy work with convicts and asserted that lack of parental involvement and childhood brokenness appeared to him as the primary cause of unhealthy pursuit of damaging relationships.

Another important aspect to be included in Islamic school curriculum and textbook is the importance of ***'social media'***. We know social media as many different forms like magazines, the internet forums, the web blogs, the blogs, the social blogs, the wikis, the social networks (facebook, whatsapp, twitter), podcasts, photos, videos, the ratings, social books social media etc. It is the interaction amongst people in which they create, share or exchange information and ideas in virtual communities and networks. Islam has indeed given a very great importance to social interaction but within limits and for the right reasons. Islam appreciates and welcomes all forms of advancement for as long as it does not go against Islam and the teachings of Muhammad (peace be upon him).

If you take a look at the word 'social', Mufti Ismail Menk in his social blog has beautifully explained how this technology has given birth to ***Social media orphans***, these social networking sites and the social media is the cause of the snatching away of the peace of a lot of people. Parents are complaining about how their spouse is not paying attention and children are complaining about their parent's addiction to social media. Social Media is just being used for online shopping, online games and sharing images and messages. Students in schools should be taught and trained how to use this technology effectively so that it improves their learning process.

A forum on Islamic education has come up with the Abu Dhabi Declaration (2006), an initiative taken by the UAE to upgrade the Islamic curriculum taught in schools. Dr Hassan, Minister of Education, commented on Islamic curriculum as containing contradictory ideas and did not encourage creativity. "It depends only on studying by heart without critical understanding. It is also a curriculum that depends on preaching and emotional speech, and this kind of approach cannot build a stable mentality that deals with the values of Islam logically."

What we need, the Islamic Curriculum is inculcating the democratic type of thinking in students of all ages or in other words,

'Pluralistic thinking'. The Muslim community must change the way they view Pluralistic thinking, and that they should view it in light of co-existence. The importance of co-existing and the mandatory need for tolerance and acceptance is needed in the Muslim Ummah and also acceptance of others in today's society. Training the future generation in the acceptance of human beings first and character formation should be the top priority in Islamic curriculum.

Conclusion

Curriculum development matters a lot in setting the direction of change in an organization, not only at the micro but also at macro levels. As long as the goals and objectives of curriculum development are clear in the planner's mind, cutting-edge achievements in various concerns can be realized. Curriculum is like a 'secret garden' not only for policymakers but also in school. It comes to driving improvement. In a nutshell, a newly integrated Islamic curriculum and subject matter for contemporary Islamic schools need to be devised urgently to promote Islamic identity solidarity for the Ummah. It is for the need of the young generations to be instilled with pure Islamic values and beliefs from the beginning in a very comprehensive, critical and creative manner by using newly revised integrated and dynamic approach to education. It is now time to place heavy emphasis on teaching Islam to the students through different co-curricular activities and also with the help of educational technology. This will help in sustaining the interest and intrinsically motivating them to learn. The textbooks provided in schools should infuse deep spirituality which moves those who read it, rather than being a dry academic. The sole purpose for Islamic education and framing its curriculum is to reform the young Muslim mind and not the religion Islam.

REFERENCES

Ahmadi A. (2001). *Principles and methods of training in Islam,* in Isfahan University Publishing.

Fazlur Rahman (1996). *Islam and Modernity: Transformation of an Intellectual Tradition.*

Freda Shamma, *Designing an Islamic Multi-Cultural Social Studies Course of Study,* Ed.D. Dissertation, University of Cincinnati, 1980 quoted in

Linda D. Askak, *Administration of Islamic Private Schools: A Comparative Study between Malaysia and the Philippines,* M.ed. thesis, (Kuala Lumpur: IIUM, 1996), 4748.

Ghazali Basri (1989). "Locke's Epistemological Theory and Its Implication on Western Educational Thought: an Islamic Critique," *Jurnal Pendidikan Islam,* Vol. 2: (1), (Kajang, Malaysia, ABIM, 1989). 66-67.

Hisham Altalib (2013). *Parent-Child Relations: A Guide to Raising Children.*

Ibrahem Narongraksakhet (1995). Towards an Integrated Curriculum in Islamic Private Schools in Southern Thailand: A Study on the Relationship between Traditional and Modern Subjects, M.ed thesis, (IIUM, 1995), 41.

Ismail Raji Al-Faruqi (1982). *Islamization of Knowledge: Problems, Principles and Prospective,* (Herndon USA: International Institute of Islamic Thought, 1982).

Linda D. Askak (1996). *Administration of Islamic Private Schools: A Comparative Study between Malaysia and the Philippines,* M.ed.thesis, (Kuala Lumpur: IIUM, 1996), 47-48.

Mufti Ismail Menk (2014). https://www.institutealislam.com/islam-and-social-media

Rosnani Hashim (1996). Elaborates in her book entitled; *Educational Dualism in Malaysia*, (Kuala Lumpur: Oxford University Press, 1996), 9-12.

Shahed Ali (1994). "Conflict between religion and secularism in the modern world and the role of education in preserving, transmitting and promoting Islamic culture", *Muslim Education Quarterly,* Vol. 2 (1), (United Kingdom, The Islamic Academy, 1984). 51-57.

Susan Douglass, Ann El-Moslimany, and Sommieh Uddin (2005). "Modelling Methods for Integrated Curriculum—Three Teaching Units" paper presented at ISNA Education Forum 2005, Chicago, (28 May 2005).

Syed Muhammad Naquib Al-Attas (1991). *The Concept of Education in Islam.* (Kuala Lumpur: The International Institute of Islamic Thought and Civilization, 1991). *Aims and Objectives of Islamic Education Islam and Secularism,* (Kuala Lumpur: Muslim Youth Movement Malaysia, 1978).

Refer to al-Qur'an: Surah Al-Hujurat 49:10 and At-Taubah 9:71.

7

Islamic Curriculum: Origin and Meaning

Madiha Parvez

The word curriculum derives from a Latin word "currere" which means "a race" or "the course of a race".

The word came first in use by University of Paris in 1576. The word curriculum covers whole academic content of a school, college and university. Generally curriculum refers to the knowledge and skills, that students achieve in a given time in given circumstances. It covers the lesson taught by teacher, assignments given by the teachers and the projects as well and it also covers the various assessment methods used by the teacher to evaluate student teaching and learning process in a particular course.

In simple terms, curriculum explains as a total experience gained by a student in an educational process that have a planned and sequential form of instruction that leads to progress and achievement in students' personality. Curriculum development plays a great role as it a planned, a purposeful, progressive and systematic process to create desirable improvement in existing educational system.

Curriculum is a means to achieve the aims of education which are dynamic and go on with the changing social requirements.

General Definitions of Curriculum

- A course of study that will enable the learner to acquire specific knowledge and skills.
- A detailed plan for instruction set by policymakers.
- A selection of information, segregated into disciplines and courses, typically designed to achieve a specific educational objective.

- Curriculum includes everything that takes place, and everything that does not take place, within the purview of the school.

Wholesome Explanation of Definitions

As a curriculum being a vital part of an educational process, plays a great role. It gives an appropriate opportunity to students to gain knowledge of all domains of life. A correct selection of knowledge, skills and information in a planned set of instruction given by the teachers to achieve all desirable educational objectives in a set time.

Definitions by Eminent Scholars

- **Ralph Tyler (1957):** "The curriculum is all of learning of students which is planned by and directed by school to attain its educational goals."
- **Peter F. Olivia (1989):** "The programme, a plan a content and learning experience."
- **Johnson (1967):** "Curriculum is a structural services of intended learning outcomes. Curriculum prescribes (or at least anticipates) result of instruction. It does not prescribe the means.... To be used in achieving the results."
- **Musgrave (1968):** "The contrived activity and experience organised, focused, systematic– that life, unaided, would not provide."
- **Ronald Doll (1970):** "The curriculum is now generally considered to be all of the experience that learners have under the auspices of that school."

Need and Importance of Curriculum

A curriculum is considered the "heart" of any learning institution which means that any institute cannot exist without a curriculum.

Curriculum as a backbone for any course to be studied in any institute, whether it is School, College or University. As our society is changing day by day and to cover up these changes, a proper framework of curriculum to be implemented in formal education system. In broadest sense, Curriculum stands as a total learning experiences of individuals not only in school but in society as well.

There is a also need to update the curriculum time to time because the needs and demands of the society are fastly changing day by day.

Curriculum development gives better way to improve the economy of a country. It provides answer and solutions to the world's pressing conditions and problems.

Curriculum is in fact the warp and woof of the whole educational process. It covers content activities and experiences in the properly graded form.

An effective curriculum gives a teacher student, administrators and society. It covers content activities and experiences in the properly graded form.

An effective curriculum gives a teacher student, administrators and society a measurable plan and structure to deliver a better qualitative education.

Types of Curriculum

Following types of curricula are used mainly in educational Institutions:

- Integrated curriculum
- Core Curriculum
- Teacher centred curriculum
- Learner centred curriculum
- Activity experience curriculum

Integrated curriculum

Described as one that connects different areas of study by cutting across subject matter lines and emphasizing unifying concepts. Integration focuses on making connections for students, allowing them to engage in relevant, meaningful activities that can be connected to real life.

The Integrated Curriculum Model (ICM) is a path to teach and deal with gifted students in such a way that is sensitive to their needs. This model gives an emphasis on advance content knowledge, relies on higher order thinking skills, and focuses learning on major issues that cross a number of subjects.

Curriculum can give the platform for developing critical thinking in students and facilitating them to remain busy in their own learning. An integrated curriculum or interdisciplinary curriculum is a type of curriculum in which relevant sources of content from different sections are combined cutting across learning subject-matter borderlines and giving due emphasis on unifying concepts. The most important function of integrated curriculum is to make students able to engage in relevant and meaningful learning activities which help to connect them to their own real life situations and the other world. This requires the combination of cooperative learning and problem-solving skills as an essential part of the curriculum.

Significance

I remember learning in the classroom and being taught subjects in isolation. For example, I was only taught reading comprehension in reading class or math in only mathematics class but never in other subjects. I often wondered why some math concepts were not taught in science since they somehow seemed to have a relationship.

Core Curriculum

The core curriculum is the set of common courses required of all undergraduates and considered the necessary general education for students, irrespective of their choice in major. It is not only academically rigorous but psychologically sound.

Significance

It plays a great role in approaching college level studies. Core curriculum helps for successful future of students.

Teacher Centred Curriculum

Teachers participate in a variety of curriculum activities at classroom level. These are the very core of their daily teaching tasks and include such activities as selection of specific content, selection of teaching.

Significance

It becomes very easy for the teacher to achieve desired goals and in this type subject matter is logically arranged because of the teachers contribution subject content is psychologically sound.

Learner Centred Curriculum

This type of curriculum emphasizes on students learning and experience and curriculum is organized according to the need and interest of students. Learner here is at central position and starts their learning from their own experiences. Teacher only work as a guide here.

Significance

It is the most important form of curriculum and it plays a great role in shaping personality of students according to their rate of development and intelligence

Activity Centred Curriculum

It is also called as project or an experience curriculum. Activity is used as a media or means of imparting knowledge and skills Activity is the greatest motivation for the child because children take interest in doing something and gain something from doing have a long lasting impact on children mind.

Significance

Problem solving strategy is one of the best techniques used in activity based curriculum. Teacher and student altogether plan the activities.

Islam and Education

Islam is an Abrahamic monotheistic religion teaching that there is only one God (Allah) and that Muhammad (s.a.w.) is the messenger of Allah. It is the world's second largest religion and the fastest growing major religion in the world with over 1.8 billion followers or 24.1 per cent of the global population, known as Muslim.

Islam means "Submission to the will of God" adherents of Islam are called Muslims.

Islam emphasize on giving and talking education. "Seek knowledge from the cradle to the grave and search for knowledge is the duty of every Muslim. Verily Allah loves the seekers of knowledge."

"Never feel ashamed to learn something you do not know."

"Knowledge is the only thing that when given it does not decrease."

The first world revealed to our Prophet Muhammad (P.B.U.H) from Allah s.w.t was "Iqra" which means to read!, to seek knowledge!, Educate yourself! Be educated.

"IQRA BISMI RABBIKAL-LAZI KHALAQ"

Need and Importance of Islamic Curriculum in School

At secondary level: The main aim of Islamic education at secondary level is to spread Islam to aware the students about practice of Islam religion. Principles and beliefs of Islam taught best through education. This leads to opening of Maktabs where the study of Holy Qur'an becomes a prominent feature. These institutions were built near the Mosque where theological thinking could flourish to the maximum level.

As we have hard and strict rules and regulations to govern the life of Gurukul students as we had very strict rules in Maktabs and Madarsah that develop a well-balanced personality. Islamic curriculum is of more importance as it develops a student perfectly in all field of life. Islamic values give a well-defined path for a student to move on it. Islamic education teaches the difference between right and wrong in life. As secondary school level covers the adolescence age and this is a sensitive stage of one's life, so balanced teaching of Islam regularly to the students make them well cultured, well-adjusted and well enough mature to take decisions of life.

REFERENCES

http://en.m.wikipedia.org>wiki>curriculum
http://www.edglossary.org>curriculum

www.udel.edu>educ>whitson>files
www.homoeofbob.com
simplyeducate.me>2014/12/13>the-meaning
www.preservearticles.com
http://research-education-edu.blogspot.com
www.publishyourarticles.net
http://www.quora.com
http:en.m.wikipedia.org>wiki>islam
http://classroom.synonyms.com>importence

8

Teaching in Islam: Innovative Methods

Nasrin

Education has been always a major concern of the Muslim world. It was launched by the Prophet Muhammad who was not only the preacher of a new religion and the head of the new community, but also an effective teacher and an enthusiastic promoter of learning. Islam is a knowledge-based religion, a religion of the Book. Since Muslim civilization has religion as a unifying factor, it is naturally based on the Qur'an and the tradition (Hadith). As soon as the Masjid became the place of worship, it also became the first school in Islam and the main place for spreading Islamic education. Education as a profession was approached by the Arabs seriously and with great care and zeal. They tried to understand the nature and the capabilities of their pupils and examined the teachers' responsibility for making learning happen.

Meaning of Innovative Methods

Innovation can be defined simply as a "new idea, device or method". However, innovation is often also viewed as the application of better solutions that meet new requirements, unarticulated needs, or existing market needs.

Innovative teaching is necessary for the present and future of education to help students to reach their full potential. Higher education should serve the long term intellectual needs of the student, for example, whether providing new material by teachers helped the student to gain new insights or opened up new channels of intellectual stimulation or enhanced student's essential and creative thinking power? Innovative teaching is necessity for all teachers in order to meet the educational needs of the new generations. However, teachers' competency for innovative teaching is a key factor influencing innovative teaching performance. Some research point out that many teachers lack competencies for innovative teaching.

List of Innovative Methods

1. Project method
2. Demonstration method
3. Brainstorming
4. Discussion method
5. Mnemonics method
6. Play way method
7. Reflection method
8. Gamification method
9. Z to A approach

Project Method in Islamic Education

In Islamic education Project method is one of the modern methods of teaching in which, the students' point of view is given importance in designing the curricula and content of studies. This method is based on the philosophy of Pragmatism and the principle of 'Learning by doing'. It demands work from the pupils. It takes the students beyond the walls of the classroom. It is carried out in a natural setting, thus making learning realistic and experiential.

The project method is a medium of instruction which was introduced during the 18th century into the schools of architecture and engineering in Europe when graduating students had to apply the skills and knowledge they had learned in the course of their studies to problems they had to solve as practicians of their trade, for example, designing a monument, building a steam engine. In the early 20th Century, William Heard Kilpatrick expanded the project method into a philosophy of education. His device is child-centred and based in progressive education. Both approaches are used by teachers worldwide to this day. Unlike traditional education, proponents of the project method attempt to allow the student to solve problems with as little teacher direction as possible. The teacher is seen more as a facilitator than a delivery of knowledge and information.

Students in a project method environment should be allowed to explore and experience their environment through their senses and, in a sense, direct their own learning by their individual interests. Very little is taught from textbooks and the emphasis is on experiential learning, rather than rote and memorization. A project method classroom focuses on democracy and collaboration to solve "purposeful" problems.

Advantages of Project Method in Islamic Education

1. It helps in developing social norms and social values among the learners.
2. It provides invaluable opportunities for correlation of various elements of the subject matter and for transfer of training or learning.
3. It helps in growing knowledge very effectively as a result of their close cooperation on social participation in the spirit of democracy.

Disadvantages of Project Method in Islamic Education

1. The project cannot be planned for all subjects and whole subject matter cannot be taught by this strategy.
2. It is not economical from the point of view of time and cost.

3. It is very difficult for a teacher to plan or to execute the projects to the learners and supervise them.

Demonstration Method in Islamic Education

Demonstration method is a teaching method used to communicate an idea with the aid of visuals such as flip charts, posters, power point, etc. A demonstration is the process of teaching someone how to make or do something in a step-by-step process. As you show how, you "tell" what you are doing.

Demonstration involves showing by reason or proof, explaining or making clear by use of examples or experiments. Put more simply, demonstration means 'to clearly show' teaching through demonstration, students are set up to potentially conceptualize class material more effectively as shown in a study which specifically focuses on chemistry demonstrations presented by teachers. Demonstrations often occur when students have a hard time connecting theories to actual practice or when students are unable to understand application of theories.

In this method, teacher shows all the activities given in the lesson to the students as an action and explains the important points before them during demonstration. A teacher follows three steps here.

I. In the first step he introduces the lesson by question-answer or lecture method.

II. In the second step he demonstrates each and every aspect of the lesson and develops it by his activities. For example, if he is teaching the characteristics of CO_2, he will show how it extinguishes the fire or how it turns lime water milky.

III. In the third step, he makes the student drill of the subject-matter for the purpose of assimilation. He asks evaluative questions here. Thus, desired skill is developed in students by imitation of action.

Advantages of Demonstration Method in Islamic Education

1. This method of teaching serves as model laboratory instruction.
2. Experiment shown as demonstration points out this matter of observation and indicates this inference.
3. It makes the pupils familiar with the nature and use of apparatus.
4. Experiments requiring special skill will merely be shown by the teacher. In this method no time is wasted.
5. Teacher's time is properly utilized in watching the students doing experiments.
6. While doing practical, there remains no necessity for explaining except educating precautions.
7. This method proves more useful if the pupils are told beforehand that they are going to do practical in the laboratory.

Disadvantages of Demonstration Method in Islamic Education

1. There is danger of students being dishonest when teacher has to play the main role in the discussion and demonstration of the topic.
2. Teachers may be tempted to lecture rather than to teach.
3. Teachers do not try for more experiments than those given in the textbook prescribed.
4. Oral discussion may not be encouraged, since it will go to restrict the demonstration experiment.
5. Practical as required may not go hand in hand with demonstration work.

Suggestion

A teacher while using this method of teaching should keep the following suggestions into his mind.

i. Teacher should prepare well what and how he has to demonstrate in the class.
ii. Students should be given enough chance to remove their doubts after the demonstration of the lesson is over.
iii. After the teacher's activity is over, students should be asked to repeat the demonstration for the purpose of drill.
iv. Important points should be explained by delivering short lectures during the process of demonstration.
v. The total demonstration process should be divided into different phases and students should be continuously evaluated after every phase.

Brainstorming in Islamic Education

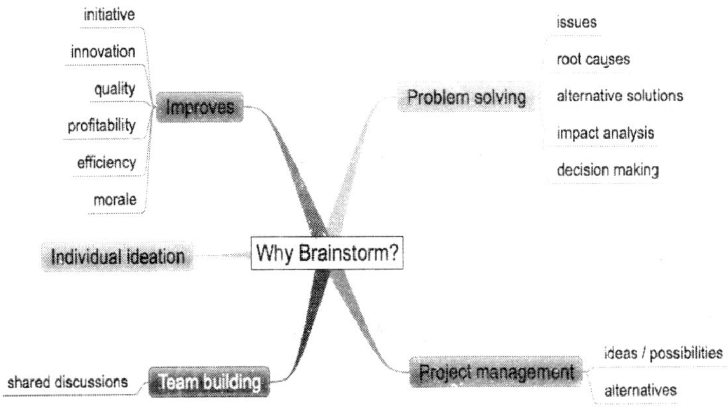

Brainstorming is a large or small group activity that encourages students to focus on a topic and contribute to the free flow of ideas. The teacher may begin a brainstorming session by posing a question or a problem, or by introducing a topic. Students then express possible answers, relevant words and ideas.

Brainstorming in Islamic education is a group creativity technique by which efforts are made to find a conclusion for a specific problem by gathering a list of ideas spontaneously contributed by its members.

In other words, brainstorming is a situation where a group of people meet to generate new ideas and solutions around a specific domain of interest by removing inhibitions. People are able to think more freely and they suggest many spontaneous new ideas as possible.

Brainstorming is a strategy used to generate a number of ideas to help solve a particular problem. The technique has been around for over 70 years and is still used today to engage students in solving a range of problems. Techniques vary but there is a general structure to follow when developing brainstorming sessions. After the problem or issue is presented, students are organized into groups to brainstorm all possible ideas which could solve the problem. Discussion of these ideas takes place after the brainstorming session ends, usually after a defined period of time.

Brainstorming is a large or small group activity that encourages students to focus on a topic and contribute to the free flow of ideas. The teacher may begin a brainstorming session by posing a question or a problem, or by introducing a topic. Students then express possible answers, relevant words and ideas.

Advantages of Brainstorming in Islamic Education

Brainstorming is a creative process that can be undertaken individually but is mainly used in a group setting and used for creative childrens only. It is used to work through ideas to find a solution to a problem. It is a powerful way to generate, share and maximize new ideas. Brainstorming provides many advantages to the process of sorting through problems.

Creative Thinking is Encouraged

In the brainstorming method we give a problem to a group of students and say, “let’s throw some ideas out here” it gets the creative flow of ideas. Ideas give birth to more ideas and students will bounce ideas off one another. The creativity will bubble over. In brainstorming thoughts were given free rein, through this we can come up with solutions.

All Ideas are Accepted

In the brainstorming session all ideas are accepted, because of this people can afford or in a position to put forth their ideas to the group without the fear of failure.

Everyone Participates in the Brainstorming Session

In the brainstorming method every student of the group feels like part of the team. It encourages widespread participation and involvement of the student of the group. Every student's ideas are respected and valued. When solutions to problem are found, it becomes a group achievement.

Curiosity of Everyone to Find a Solution

In the brainstorming session every student is curios to find a solution to thc problcm or we can say that there is active participation in the brainstorming session.

Disadvantages of Brainstorming Method

Fearful for Introverts

Introvert students hesitate to express their ideas in a brainstorming. They feel uncomfortableness in the brainstorming method.

Group-think and Social Anxiety

Rather than focusing on generating thoughtful, original ideas, team members may be tempted by the environment to focus more on evaluating each other's ideas prematurely and making decisions rather than generating new ideas or experience social anxiety around voicing risky or unpopular ideas.

Time Pressure is not Conducive to Great Ideas

Certain bodies of research suggests that time alone with one's thoughts is important to generate real breakthroughs. Brainstorming sessions are often pressure-filled and focus on volume of ideas rather than quality.

Heuristic Method in Islamic education

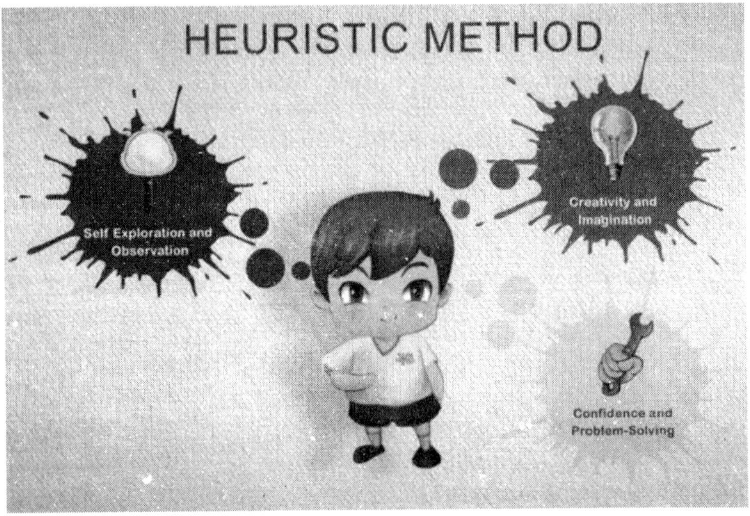

This method was first used by Professor Armstrong for teaching science. Its success led it to be adopted in the teaching of all subjects in the curriculum. The word curriculum 'heuristic' is derived from the Greek word "heurisco" (I find out) and the heuristic method is one in which the pupil are left to find out things for themselves. The children are placed, as far as possible, in the position of discoveries and instead of being told the facts, they are made to find them out for themselves. The pupil is made to learn through his own effort. He has to obtain information through books, apparatus or the teacher. But in the processing of receiving information he is not passive. Thus in this method, directing imparting of information is reduced to the smallest possible extent, but it does not mean that there is no need of teacher. He/she are there to give the children a proper start.

The word 'Heuristic' means to discover. In this method, the students be put in the place of an independent discoverer. The teacher sets a problem for the students and then asks them to discover the answer. Students find out the solution by experiments, group discussions, or any other means.

Advantages of Heuristic method in Islamic Education

It helps in achieving cognitive, affective and psychomotor objectives i.e. it helps in all round development of the child.

1. Students are put into the situation to learn by self-experience. It certainly develops self-confidence and self-reliance in the learners.
2. It helps in developing scientific attitude and creativity in the learners.
3. Teacher encourages the learners to explore the environment in search of the solution of the problems. By doing so, some new knowledge is discovered by them.
4. Teacher is always ready to provide individual guidance regarding the solution of the problem. Thus, interaction between the teacher and the learner takes place in a cooperative, conducive environment.

Disadvantages of Heuristic Teaching Method in Islamic Education

1. It cannot be used at primary level of education.
2. Higher intelligence and divergent thinking is required in the learners. But, there are some students who are below average and fail to succeed in discovering the solutions of the problems. It frustrates them.
3. In true sense, none of the teachers have patience for providing individual guidance to the learners. And learners, too, feel hesitation to approach the teacher for seeking his help.

Suggestions

1. There can be number of solutions for a problem. So, it is the teacher's duty to provide guidance to the learners to select the most relevant solution of the problem.
2. Problem should be related to the course and curriculum and

a definite time period should be allotted to the learners to finish their research work.

3. Students' abilities, capabilities, interest and choice of the subject should be taken into consideration in allotting the problems.
4. There should be eligibility criteria for providing the problems.

Gamification in Islamic Education

The Gamification of learning is an educational approach to motivate students to learn by using video game design and game elements in learning environments. The goal is to maximize enjoyment and engagement through capturing the interest of learners and inspiring them to continue learning. Gamification, broadly defined, is the process of defining the elements which comprise games that make those games fun and motivate players to continue playing, and using those same elements in a non-game context to influence behaviour. There are two forms of Gamification—structural with no subject matter changes, and the altered content method that adds subject matter. Games applied in learning can be considered as serious games, where the learning experience is centred around serious stories. The serious story is "impressive in quality" and "part of a thoughtful process" to achieve learning goals.

Advantages of Gamification in Islamic Education

Improves knowledge absorption and retention:

Students develop and practice problem-solving strategies across different levels of play or contexts.

Provides immediate feedback to help players adjust to learning challenges:

Sum dog is an online gaming programme that reinforces math and language arts skills, players receive automatic feedback when a question is answered, at the end of a level corrective feedback is given to the players.

Disadvantages of Gamification in Islamic Education

Requires access to computer and Internet

- School do not have budget available to purchase computers.
- Students of low-income families may not have technology available to them in the home to support learning.
- Poor design in game leads to disengagement and confusion.
- Teacher fails to implement gaming to effectively support curriculum and learning.
- Students manage time poorly because they are determined to pass a certain level in an online game.

Reflective Teaching in Islamic Education

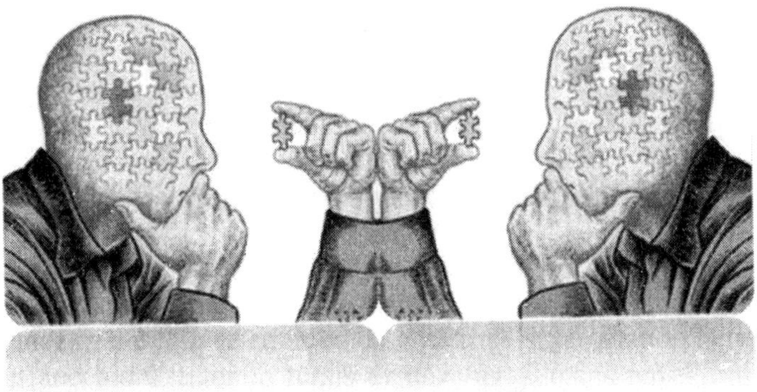

Reflective teaching is a process where teachers think over their teaching practices, analyzing how something was taught and how the practice might be improved or changed for better learning outcomes. Some points of consideration in the reflection process might be what is currently being done, why it is being done and how well students are learning. You can use reflection as a way to simply learn more about your own practice, improve a certain practice (small groups and cooperative learning, for example) or to focus on a problem students are having.

Approaches to Critical Reflection

Peers Observation—Peers observation can provide opportunities for teachers to view each other's teaching in order to expose them to different teaching styles and to provide opportunities for critical reflection on their own teaching. Some suggestions for peer observation are:

1. Each participant would both observe and be observed. Teachers would work in pairs and take turns observing each other's classes.
2. Pre-observation orientation session: Prior to each observation, the two teachers would meet to discuss the nature of the class to be observed, the kind of material being taught, the teachers' approach to teaching, the kinds of students in the class, typical patterns of interaction and class participation, and any problems that might be expected. The teacher being observed would also assign the observer a goal for the observation and a task to accomplish. The task would involve collecting information about some aspect of the lesson, but would not include any evaluation of the lesson. Observation procedures or instruments to be used would be agreed upon during this session and a schedule for the observations arranged.
3. The observation: The observer would then visit his or her partner's class and complete the observation using the procedures that both partners had agreed on.
4. Post-observation: The two teachers would meet as soon as possible after the lesson. The observer would report on the information that had been collected and discuss it with the teacher (Richards and Lockhart, 1991).

Advantages of Reflection Method in Islamic Education

The teachers identify a variety of different aspects of their lessons for their partners to observe and collect information. These include organization of the lesson, teacher's time management, students' performance on tasks, time-on-task, teacher questions and student responses, student performance during pair work, classroom interaction, class performance during a new teaching activity, and students' use of the first language or English during group work. The teachers gain a number of insights about their own teaching from their colleague's observations and that they would like to use peer observation on a regular basis. They may also obtain new insights into aspects of their teaching.

Written Accounts of Experiences

Another useful way of engaging in the reflective process is through the use of written accounts of experiences (Powell 1985) and their potential is increasingly being recognized in teacher education. A number of different approaches can be used.

Self-Reports: Self-reporting involves completing an inventory or check-list in which the teacher indicates which teaching practices were used within a lesson or within a specified time period and how often they were employed (Pak, 1985).

Self-reporting allows teachers to make a regular assessment of what they are doing in the classroom. They can check to see to what extent their assumptions about their own teaching are reflected in their actual teaching practices.

Journal Writing

A procedure which is becoming more widely acknowledged as a valuable tool for developing critical reflection is the journal or diary. The goals of journal writing are:

1. To provide a record of the significant learning experiences that have taken place.
2. To help the participant come into touch and keep in touch with the self-development process that is taking place for them.

3. To provide the participants with an opportunity to express, in a personal and dynamic way, their self-development.
4. To foster a creative interaction between the participant and the self-development process that is taking place, between the participant and other participants who are also in the process of self-development, between the participant and the facilitator whose role is to foster such development. (Powell, 1985, Bailey, 1990)

Recording Lessons

For many aspects of teaching, audio or video recording of lessons can also provide a basis for reflection. While there are many useful insights to be gained from diaries and self-reports, they cannot capture the moment to moment processes of teaching. Many things happen simultaneously in a classroom, and some aspects of a lesson cannot be recalled. It would be of little value for example, to attempt to recall the proportion of Yes-No Questions to WH-Questions a teacher used during a lesson, or to estimate the degree to which teacher time was shared among higher and lower ability students. Many significant classroom events may not have been observed by the teacher, let alone remembered, hence the need to supplement diaries or self-reports with recordings of actual lessons.

Conclusion

Reflective teaching involves changes in the way we usually perceive teaching and our role in the process of teaching. Teachers who explore their own teaching through critical reflection develop changes in attitudes and awareness which they believe can benefit their professional growth as teachers, as well as improve the kind of support they provide their students. Like other forms of self-inquiry, reflective teaching is not without its risks, since journal writing, self-reporting or making recordings of lessons can be time-consuming. However teachers engaged in reflective analysis of their own teaching report that it is a valuable tool for self-evaluation and professional growth. Reflective teaching suggests that experience alone is insufficient for professional growth, but that experience coupled with reflection can be a powerful impetus for teacher development.

You might find, as you progress, that there is an area of knowledge you need to know more about. So never be afraid to ask for help or advice. There is nothing wrong with asking, "How can I do it better?" Doing this is not a sign of being an underwhelming teacher; in fact it is quite the opposite: It shows you are brave and professional.

Mnemonics Method in Islamic Education

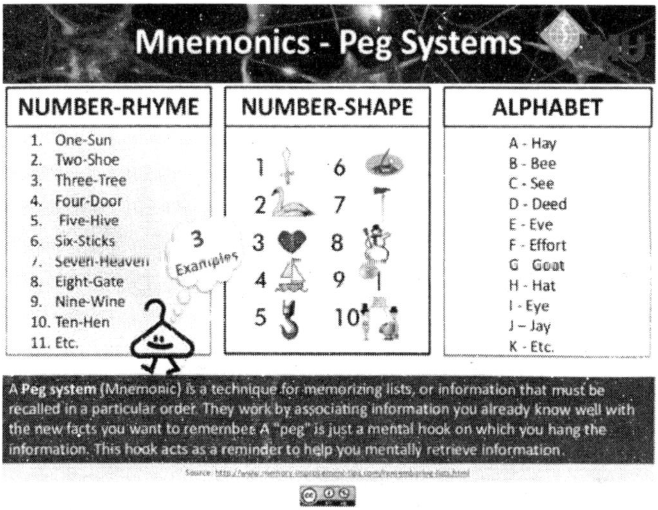

Mnemonic method or memory device is a learning technique that aids information retention or retrieval (remembering) in the human memory. Mnemonics make use of elaborative encoding, retrieval cues, and imagery as specific tools to encode any given information in a way that allows for efficient storage and retrieval. Mnemonics aid original information in becoming associated with something more accessible or meaningful. Mnemonics method provides better retention of the information. Commonly encountered mnemonics are often used for lists and in auditory form, such as short poems, acronyms, or memorable phrases, verses of holy Qur'an, prayer etc., but mnemonics can also be used for other types of information and in visual or kinesthetic forms. Their use is based on the observation that the human mind more easily remembers spatial, personal, surprising, physical, sexual, humorous, or otherwise "relatable" information, rather than more abstract or impersonal forms of information.

Advantages of Mnemonics Method

Mnemonics are fun tools or memory aids you can use to remember word sequence. Figures, events, face and facts, can be mastered and recalled by using memory aids, popularly known as mnemonics. In fact, using mnemonics is effective compared to other conventional means such as repetition and rote learning.

Discussion Method in Islamic Education

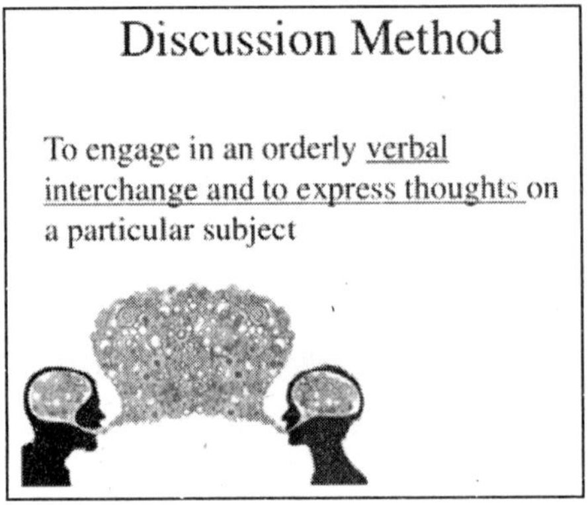

Discussion methods are a variety of forums for open-ended, collaborative exchange of ideas among a teacher and student or among students for the purpose of furthering students thinking, learning, problem solving, understanding, or literary appreciation.

It is also an oral method like question answer method and maximum interaction between a teacher and students can be seen here. Discussion can be formal as well as informal. Formal discussion can be arranged for the purpose of achieving predetermined objectives. In that case rules of the discussions are also predetermined. On the other hand, informal discussions are neither objectives oriented nor rules are predetermined. Teacher and student discuss the issue in the class whenever it becomes necessary.

In formal discussion teacher divides the class into different groups and give the topic of discussion to the each group. Every group has a leader to anchor and conducts the discussion. It is the leader who raises new topics of discussion. In the end, teacher draws the conclusion of the discussion with the help of leaders. Thus we see that students are more active in the class through this method of teaching. Teacher plays the role of a guide or helper only.

Suggestions

1. Efforts should be made to motivate all the students to take part in the discussion. Even mute students should be encouraged to actively take part in the discussion. Students criticize one another during discussion in the class. A teacher should accept only those criticisms which are really logical and meaningful.
2. Students should anchor the discussion themselves. Teacher should be there in the class only as a guide.
3. A teacher should select the topic for discussion only with help of student.
4. Students who have leadership qualities should be selected for the anchoring.
5. Only those topics should be selected for the discussion which has any relevance to the life of the students.

Advantages of Discussion Method

a. Thinking and communicating powers of the students can be developed through this method.
b. Leadership qualities can be developed through this method.
c. The expression abilities of the students can be developed through this method.
d. Here students find out the solution of the problem themselves. It develops the creative potential of the students.
e. The attitudes and interest of student can be drawn out towards learning through this method.
f. Higher level cognitive and affective objectives can be realized through classroom discussions.

9

Methods of Education and Teaching in Islam

Aquib Akhtar

What were the methods of teaching and instruction in Islam and how did the Qur'an deal with these methods and in what style? Was the teaching teacher centred or pupil-centred? A-Z studied the different methods, and even alludes to the education of women, a subject most neglected in those times. In those days, the purpose of education was to spread religion by enabling people to read the Qur'an. As Ibn Khaldoon (1332-1406 AD) says: "The Qur'an is the principle of all religious education", including reading and writing (Subh, 1993, Vol. 1, pp. 356-357, 429). While in the first years of the Islam, there were private teachers who only taught the children of the Caliphs and other wealthy pupils, in the Abbasid era (750-1258) scholars became widely appreciated by society. Scholars sought higher education to gain high status and respect, but they also worked in small jobs to earn a living. For example, the poet Abu al-'Atahiya was a ceramic artist, al-Jahiz was a bread-seller and fishmonger and al-Ghazali's name refers to his father's job as a worker in the production of woolen clothes (Ahmad, 1989, p. 39). A-Z stated that "in the ancient time" teaching was free: "In ancient times people learned handicrafts, then they pursued the study of knowledge so that they did not desire the possessions of men" (*Ibid.*, p. 147). However, when Islam spread, education and teaching became established and the teachers began to earn money. Since the mosque, the first educational centre for the study of the Qur'an and religious thought, was not a suitable place for children, separate institutions, Kuttabs, were established for them. When A-Z wrote his book, organized education was at a high level. From that time on, the importance of education and the pursuit of knowledge were emphasized in the Islamic faith. At first imitation was the common method of education. The child who saw his parents read the holy Qur'an and observe religious rites was supposed to pick up these activities and repeat them. Islam's pedagogical approach of the pre-medieval and medieval ages was an almost completely religious approach, as was likewise the case in those times in the Christian West. A-Z refers largely to pleasures derived from doing one's duty to the Islamic religion. But he also noted that learned men have fame and that their learning continues to live after they die, and they are remembered as important people. In the pre-medieval periods, the traditional method of teaching prevailed. Learning was based on recitation and on the teacher's personal style and his ability to explain and interpret the texts as well as the pupil's ability to memorize them. The Qur'an had to be memorized by every child. The extensive use of memory was an important feature of the Arab learning method. Repetitions and memory drills were recommended and frequently used. Modern researchers assert that Islamic scholars were interested in methods of teaching both young and adult Muslims. Those methods were a function of the following criteria:

a. Subject
b. Teacher and scholars
c. Place of teaching
d. Age of student

A-Z explains that the teaching methods differed according to these criteria. The methods used to teach the Qur'an were not the same as the ones used to teach science, and the teachers differed in their way of instruction depending on their knowledge and preparation. The motivation of the student, his readiness to absorb new material was another reason to choose one or another method, and A-Z states that the teacher must get to know the student in order to give the best educational guidance. He also asserts that teaching children is different from adult education (Ahmad, 1989, p. 114).

The teaching methods were derived, in essence, from the Qur'an and the Hadith, i.e. tradition. A-Z therefore advises potential teachers to preach with consideration and circumspection: "I commend to you in the composing of your speech five things, if you are obedient to him who makes recommendation to you meaning you well. Do not neglect the purpose of the discourse, the time, its quality (how to speak, in low voice or loudly, quietly...), its quantity (in condense manner) and its place" (Ahmad, 1989, p. 114). The Muslims were concerned about the learning climate that accompanies the teaching process. In order to achieve better learning and results, suitable study times and places had to be chosen. As to the age at which children should start to be taught, he recommended the days of early youth and adolescence. The Qur'an urges its believers to cultivate learning and reasoning through constant exhortations, demanding that they know, see, observe, ponder and deduce. Muslims believe that God sent his messenger, the Prophet Muhammad, to be an example to people and to develop Islamic education, and A-Z stated that in the Prophet's sayings there is no limit to learning. But he also observes that the Messenger never recommends a fixed style for teaching. The teacher may switch from narration to dialogue, from interrogation to the setting of parables. Taking A-Z's book as a basis, we shall try here to offer an insight on the several methods of education that can be found in the Qur'an and the Sunna. Methods like education through preaching and counselling or direct commandment were teacher centred. These are the oldest methods. With the lapse of time there appeared newer methods, like the style of debate, the dialogue, the narrative style and the setting of parables, which were pupil-centred. A-Z observes that in the Qur'an every way of teaching was teacher-centred and based on the assumption that the Qur'an was the teacher, under the dictation of God who revealed how to act and behave. The Prophet Muhammad is considered the first teacher in Islam. He was a very able teacher who wanted his pupils to be active and learn and do things by themselves. In this he was an innovator and established new bases for Muslim teaching. Education by Preaching, Advice and Commandment. The basic method recommended in the Qur'an consists in preaching and advice. This has the most influence on the child's development from a religious, behavioural, psychological and social point of view. The educators must understand that the sensitivity of the child to preaching is great, since his heart is still innocent and not corrupted. In his book, A-Z also examines the preacher's style and his advice to the learner is: "Ask advice in all matters and be firm and exert patience with his teacher" (Ahmad, 1989, pp. 100, 102). He also says: "It is necessary to choose ...to ask advice in all matters" (*Ibid.*, pp. 98, 100). He even utters a series of commandments to the teacher and to the learner. An interesting point of view is the following: "Know that it is not obligatory for every Muslim, man or woman, to seek all aspects of learning, but only that in keeping with his situation in life ('Ilm al-Hal)"(*Ibid.*, p. 83). A-Z also proclaimed that: "It is necessary in the quest for learning not to neglect the properties and usage of the Prophet" (*Ibid.*, p. 166), and that: "It is Education and Methods of Teaching in Islam in the Era of Az-Zarnooji necessary in the quest of knowledge to be on one's guard against shameful traits of character..." (*Ibid.*, p. 115). These assumptions mean that teaching was not only knowledge, but also had a behavioural and moral aspect. The Qur'an gives a lot of advice concerning learning. Here are some commandments: "God commands justice, the doing of good, and liberality to kith and kin, and forbids all shameful deeds and injustice and rebellion. He instructs you that ye may receive admonition" (Qur'an: S. 16; V. 90, Ali, 1946). God almighty made it the responsibility of Islamic society to bring up its children by ordering them to do good and forbid them to do wrong: "Let there arise out of you a band of people who stand for all that is good, enjoining you to do what is right and forbidding what is wrong. They are the ones to attain felicity" (Qur'an: S. 3; V. 104, Ali, 1946). "Ye are the best of peoples, evolved for mankind, enjoining what is right, forbidding what is wrong, and believing" (*Ibid.*, V. 110).

Teaching by Repetition (Tikrar)

Preaching needs to be supported by repetition. Whenever Allah's messenger spoke, he repeated the words thrice, so that they might be fully understood. A-Z spoke of the amount to be repeated at any one time, thus defining the repetition method, called tikrar and its technique. The student should count and measure for himself the amount of repetition he needs. A-Z stated that "the quest of knowledge is among the most exalted and difficult tasks" (Ahmad, 1989, p. 101). He therefore urged the learners to cultivate learning and reasoning so as to acquire the knowledge already owned, according to the Qur'an, by Biblical figures such as Noah, David, Solomon and Moses. Islam has used effective styles to produce divine emotions in man and to train the human mind. The whole universe absorbed the light of Islamic culture during its years of glory and the Islamic nation led the other nations to the light of knowledge and the supremacy of morality (An-Nahlawi, 1979, pp. 184-185). This occurred thanks to the superior methods of teaching using a variety of styles, and these methods of education can be found in the Qur'an and the Sunna. The Qur'an recommended education through the persuasive approach of preaching and advice. This guidance can be done if the soul is pure, the heart is open, and the intellect is good. The educators must understand this as being most important in the education of children, and prepare the young ones for their psychological and social development, leading them towards behavioural and mental maturity.

The Narrative Method

Another very effective method of teaching described by A-Z is the narrative style. This consists in telling a story, thus making long-lasting intellectual impressions on the listener by the liveliness, the conclusion and the message of the narrative. The Qur'an uses this style especially in the stories of the apostles and their peoples. The Qur'anic stories include psychological evidence of the power and the comprehensiveness of Islam: "God granted his messenger Muhammad the best of stories and gave him the best Hadith so that the people would have an oracle and lesson, and the Prophet would have resolution and stability" ('Ulwan, 1994, Vol. 2, pp. 661-669). The educational characteristics of the prophetic stories are their ability to draw the reader in and catch his attention. A-Z quoted stories such as Harun al-Rashid, the Caliph and al-Asma'i and the tale of Yahya and that of Dhu al-Qarnayn, who is represented on his coins with two horns on his head because he considered himself a son of Jupiter Ammon (who had the horns of a ram) (Muruj ad-Dahab, 1989, Vol. 1, pp. 249-250). Dhu al-Qarnayn wished to make an expedition in order to become master of the East (rising of the sun) and the West (reaching the setting of the sun—west of Macedonia), and he become master of the East and West, therefore he called Dhu al-Qarnayn. Once he consulted learned men and asked: "Why Education and Methods of Teaching in Islam in the Era of Az-Zarnooji do I make an expedition for such an amount of empire? For verily, the world is small and perishable and rule of the world is a contemptible affair. So this expedition is not a noble way to exert oneself". But the learned men said: "Make the expedition in order that you may have possession of the present and the future world." He then replied: "This is good" (Ahmad, 1986, pp. 122-123). Now the world of Islam in general has accepted Alexander the Great, 356-323 B.C as the one meant by the epithet Dhu al-Qarnayn (Ath-Tha'alebi, 2003, Ch. Four). But some of our 'Ulamas have raised doubts about it and made other suggestions. One is that it was an earlier pre-historic king contemporary with Abraham; because they say, Dhu al-Qarnayn was a man of faith (Qur'an, S. 18, V. 88, 98). Dhu Al-Qarnayn, literally means "the Two Horned One", the King with the Two Horns, or the Lord of the Two Epochs (Ali 1946, Qur'an, Appendix vii, pp. 760-765). Who was he? The Qur'an gives us no material on which we can base positive answer. Nor is it necessary to find an answer, as the story is treated as a parable (Ath-Tha'alebi, 1999, pp. 61, 241). Popular opinion identifies Dhu al-Qarnayn with Alexander the Great. An alternative suggestion is an ancient Persian king, or a prehistoric Himyarite King. Dhu Al-Qarnayn was a most powerful king, but it was God, Who in His universal Plan, gave him power and provided him with way and means for his great work (for the story of Dhu Al-Qarnayn, see Ali, 1946, pp. 753-757, Qur'an, S. 18, V. 83-98, Appendix vii, pp. 760-765). In his teaching, A-Z used stories from the Qur'an and the Prophet's life and related narratives of his companions and followers. The Qur'anic story is an instrument for conveying the Islamic message. It differs from the legend, since its main aim is not telling a tale, but in strengthening a Muslim's belief and to educate him in correct and moral conduct. They usually imply a dilemma which is solved in favour of the believer who wins by his faith in God. They are a dramatic and intellectual tool for the teacher who can adjust the exposition of the narrative to a style that suits the mentality of the audience. An-Nahlawi (1979, pp. 210-217) explains the educational character of the Qur'anic and prophetic stories by the fact that the story draws the reader in, arrests his attention and makes him think what the story means. The reader or the listener follows the story and is impressed by its characters and themes, the role of which is to impart to him new knowledge and a sterling moral education.

The Dialogue Method

A further method used by medieval Muslim teachers and examined by A-Z is the dialogue. This is a conversation with the pupils, during which questions are asked to the purpose of drawing their attention and triggering their intellect. According to A-Z, "The usefulness of posing questions (debate) and discussing is greater than the usefulness of sheer repetition, since in this there is repetition and one more element. It is said: posing questions (debate) for an hour is better than a month of repetition" (Ahmad, 1989, p. 140). This conversation between two or more persons in the form of question and answer is held on a specific subject. However, A-Z warns that it is only possible when the discussion is conducted between persons with a just and candid nature. Not always does one of persons persuade the other to his opinion, but even then a message is forwarded and is examined by the listener. Several ways exist to make the dialogue interesting:

(a) Arousing emotions and feelings is possible by introducing the subject in a lively and realistic way.
(b) Enticing the learner to follow the discussion so that he will know the conclusion.

According to A-Z, the interrogative dialogue is one of the successful ways to persuade some of the intellectuals to enter Islam. This is what the author quotes in his book: "And indeed Abu Hanifa used to study by propounding questions and discussing them in his shop" (Ahmad, 1989, p. 143). He finds this method to be a successful and most emulated one. It is very persuasive and forces the rival to accept the proofs offered to him. He also advises the use of the debate method in the following words: "Discuss with people subjects of learning in order that you may live. Do not keep yourself away from the enlightened. It is necessary to pursue knowledge by means of discussion, argument and questioning" (Ahmad, 1989, pp. 138-139.). In his quest for teaching ways and styles, A-Z singles out the method of setting parables. This method, also utilized in other religious scriptures, such as the Bible and the Buddhist texts, has been brought to perfection by Qur'an teachers in the medieval and pre-medieval eras. It consists in approaching a new topic through an example close to the learners' comprehension or within their range of experience, by setting a parable or, in other words, drawing a comparison. The Messenger used this method and the word "parable" literally means "example" or "comparison".

Teaching by Setting Parables

The parable is a kind of metaphor, like the use of a "donkey" to symbolize a trivial and disgusting creature which carries huge tomes (heavy books) on its back but does not understand them. This comparison has been used in the Qur'an where it stands for people who falsify the signs of God. They merely became like beasts of burden that carry learning and wisdom on their backs but do not understand or profit by it. The Qur'anic description is: "The similitude of those who were charged with the (obligations of the) law, but who subsequently failed in those (obligations), is that of a donkey which carries huge tomes (but understand them not). Evil is the similitude of people who falsify the Sign of God: And God guides not people who do wrong" [Qur'an: S. 62 (Jumu'a); V. 5, Ali, 1946]. The special theme here is the need for mutual contact in the community for worship and understanding: for the spirit of the Message is for all, ignored and learned, in order that they may be purified and may learn wisdom (*Ibid.*, p. 1544). Another example offered by A-Z concerns the medical science, when he states: "The study of the science of medicine is allowed because it deals with accidental causes. Therefore its study is allowed" (Ahmad, 1989, p. 90). And to set a parable, he remarks that "the Prophet treated himself medically" (*ibid.*). The Messenger of God took the Qur'an as an example for his own conduct, and his morality was that of the Qur'an. His companions took him as an example in response to God's saying. This method of acting as a role model is one of the most successful ways of approaching Islam education with all its factors, styles and aims. The Prophet also advised talking to the people according to their level of intelligence. This is a modern educational issue, putting the student in the centre of the learning situation and giving him the leading role. The curriculum has to be built around the students' needs and interests. It is therefore clear that the parables were not a mere artistic work, but had educational and psychological aims. According to A-Z, the educator should achieve these aims by relying on Qur'anic parables for everyday situations and school activities, and by commenting on them by a description of their social and behavioural results. These parables help to better understand the meaning of the commandment, to cultivate divine emotions, and to train the mind in correct thinking and sound logical reasoning. In Islamic education, setting an example is a most successful method in teaching others. The teacher must set an example by making his actions agree with his precepts. In connection with this, the Prophet set an example in several fields, such as good morals, worship, generosity, modesty and clemency. In his book, A-Z states that it is necessary for the seeker of knowledge to ask advice in all matters, and he sets a parable that: "God commanded even his Messenger to ask counsel about all of his affairs" (Ahmad, 1989, p. 100). Though set in early days by the Prophet, this method is a modern educational issue. The parables are not a mere artistic work giving the teacher's speech a rhetorical glamour. It has educational and psychological aims, easing the comprehension and training the mind in correct thinking and sound reasoning. The Islamic educator should achieve his aims by an abundant use of Qur'anic parables and by commenting them in the spirit of his teachings.

Teaching Through Practice and Application

In A-Z's study of the learning system, a great importance is ascribed to teaching through practice and application. Teaching by the method of application affects the soul and confirms knowledge. A-Z's study shows that activities and practices are strongly and reciprocally connected with all the elements of learning. Learning activities cannot be separated from content, aims and motivation, because activities result from motivation and lead to it. Activities can cure laziness and stave off boredom. They are not conditions that lead to learning; they are learning in itself and form part of its aims and targets. Thus, comprehension activities are not different from comprehension but are comprehension itself. As emphasized in A-Z's book, learning is working with (Ahmad, 1989, p. 98). That means that learning is working, as activities are learning. In the opinion of some educators, lectures should be replaced by class exercises in which there is a large share of student participation (Knowles, 1986, p. 37). Learning by practice and application was already for the medieval teacher a condition for accurate learning and its acceptance by God. The students see the things that they learn in a more detailed way. Quoting Abu Hanifa, A-Z said that: "The purpose of learning is to act by it, while the purpose of action is the abandoning of the perishable for that which lasts forever" (Ahmad, 1979, p. 91). This means that, according to A-Z, the teacher must educate his students to achieve in their life the principles learned from him. For this purpose, he should ask them questions about real life and make sure they apply the received education in their individual and social life. The Prophet's methods of teaching included the practice and repetition. He used to pray while standing on the rostrum and his companions prayed after him. This was an example of the modeling and practicing method. According to the Hadith, the learner should repeat the reading after hearing it, so that the teacher might correct him if he makes a mistake. A-Z explains this as follows: "It is important that the student exert himself strenuously to understand what is offered by the teacher, applying intelligence and meditation as well as repetition" (Ahmad, 1989, p. 137). He also says that: "After the student understands and repeats the material, the student should reflect, meditate, and continuously pose questions to his teachers and his colleagues so as to get a firm grasp of what he is doing" (Von Grunebaum, 1947, p. 9). One suggestion was that the student should learn whatever he could remember after two repetitions of the material (*Ibid.*, pp. 8-9). The teacher should also care to make learning easy, not complicated. This principle is applied by the Messenger in his preaching. In fact, Muslim education urges the teacher to facilitate and not complicate things. Therefore, the Prophet's Friday preaches were not long. They only consisted of a few easy words. An example of learning by "application" and "practice" is given by the way the Prophet's companions learned to perform ablution and corrected each other. The books of Hadith quote some of these methods. According to the tradition, the learner must repeat the reading after hearing it, so that the teacher can correct him if he makes a mistake. The practical and actual side of the educators' work should be more important than the theoretical one. Pupils must grow up with practical thinking, which makes them like their work and respect other workers. This principle, used in modern education, appears in the Messenger's speech and deeds, as related by A-Z. We however observe that A-Z does not talk about the acquiring of motor skills, or motor learning. This side of learning was not valued at his time, as stated by Uthman, (1989, p. 99). Worship, including prayers and alms, fasting and pilgrimage is the topic of the pre-medieval and medieval teacher's work as defined by A-Z.

Teaching by the Dictation Method

A further method of teaching emphasized in A-Z's time is the dictation. This consists in bringing up the child to have noble traits and morals. A good environment and an Islamic education will give the child the highest of spiritual virtues and personal noble traits. This was stressed in more than one Hadith: "It is better for someone to educate his son than to give a measure of charity". "The best thing that a father can give his son is good manners". "Teach your children and family goodness and give them good manners" (al-Tabrizi, 1990, Vols. 1, 2). According to A-Z dictation was one of the methods of that time: "I shall dictate to you some of the things of which knowledge consists. Since the learned man is held in honour through his knowledge, knowledge of the law is the most worthy of honour" (Ahmad, 1989, pp. 128-130). For him, the way to attain knowledge is to have an inkstand on hand on every occasion, in order to write down items of scientific interest. Making notes rather than relying on memory is an important way of learning.

BIBLIOGRAPHY

Ahmad, M. (1989). *Ta'alim al-Muta'allim (The Instruction of the Learner: Method of Learning),* Cairo: Maktabat an-Nahda.

Ahmad, L. (1992). *Women and Gender in Islam: Historical Roots of Modern Debate.* N. Haven & London: Yale University Press.

Al-Ahwani, A.F. (1955). *Tarbiat al-Muslim (Education of the Muslim).* Cairo: Isa al-Babi al-Halabi and Partners.

Ali, A. Yusuf. (1946). *The Holy Qur'an: Translation and Commentary.* U.K: Islamic Propagation Centre International.

Al-Bayruti, A. (1994). *Mukhtasar Jame' Bayan al-'Lm wa-Fadlehe (Summarising the Comprehensive Book of Learning and its Merit).* Beirut: Dar al-Khair.

Hamdan, N., *et al.*, (1989). *Fi at-Turath at-Tarbawi (On the Educational Heritage).* Damascus: Dar al Ma'moon lit-Turath.

Hamidullah, M. (1979). *Introduction to Islam.* London: MWH London Publisher.

Hamilton, D. (1992). *Learning about Education in Unfinished Curriculum.* Open University Press, Philadelphia: Milton Keyness.

Hoffman, V.J. (1985). *Women and the Family in the Middle East.* Austin University of Texas Press.

Ibn Jubayr, M. (1907). *Ar-Rehla (The Travel)*. Beirut: Dar Sader. Al-Khaledi, Kh. (2002). The Educational Theory of Burhan Ad-Din Az-Zarnooji as Reflected in his Book Instructing the Learner Methods of Learning (Ph.D Thesis). University of Liverpool.

Knowles, M. (1986). *The Adult Learner: A Neglected Species*. Houston, Texas: Golf Publisher Company.

Al-Makdisi, G. (1991). *The Rise of Colleges, the Madrasa and University in Medieval Islam*. Edinburgh: Edinburgh University Press.

Massialas, B.E. and Jarrar, S.A. (1983). *Education in the Arab World*. New York: Praeger Publishers.

Al-Mas'udi, A. (1989). *Muruj Ad-Dahab*, [*Lawns* (*Plains*) *of Gold*], Vol. 1. Daral-Kitab al-'Alamiy: Ad-Dar al-Ifreeqiya.

Mernissi, F. (1991). *Women and Islam: A Historical and Theological Enquiry*. Oxford: Blackwell.

An-Nahlawi, A.R. (1979). *Usool At-Tarbiya al-Islamiyya Wa Asalibuha* (*The Principles of Islamic Education and its Methods*). Damascus: Dar Al-Fikr.

The Open University in Israel (1989). *Individual Teaching*. Ols. 1, 2, 3, 4. T-A. Qambar, M. (1987). *Derasatfi at-Tarbia al-Islamiya* (*Heritage Studies in Islamic Education*), Vol. 2. Dawha-Qatar: Dar ath-Thaqafa.

Reda, M. (1979). *Al'Arab wal-Hadara, Derasa fi al-Fikr at-Tarbawi al-Muqaren* (*The Arabs, Education and Civilization: A Study in Comparative Educational Thought*). Kuwait: al-Manhal Publishing.

Russell, A. (1794). *Natural History of Aleppo*. London: G.G.J. Robinson. Sarwar, G. *et al.* (1996). *The Muslim Educational Trust, Issues in Islamic Education*. London: Cromwell Press.

Shalaby, A. (1986). *Al-Fikr al-Islami (Muslim Thought, its Origin and Achievements)*, Vol. 2. Caziro: An-Nahda al-Masriyya.

Shalaby, A. (1987). *At-Tarbiyawat-Ta'lim fi al-Fikr al-Islami (Teaching and Education in the Islamic* Thought), Vol. 5. Cairo: An-Nahda al-Masriyya.

Ash-Sharabasi, A. (1977). *Yas'alunaka fi ad-Din wal-Hayat* (*Asking you about Religion and Life*) Beirut: Dar al-Jeel.

Subh, M. (1993). *At-Tarbiya al-Islamiya* (*Islamic Education*), Vol. 2. Beirut: Dar al-Jeel. Kalan Mahal.

Ath-Tha'alebi, A.M. (2003). *Thimar al-Qulub fi Al-Mudaf Wal-Mansub*, Section four. Sayda: al-Maktaba al-'Azeema.

Ath-Tha'alebi, A.M. (1999). Fiqh al-Lugha Wa-Asrar al-'Arabiya (*Jurisprudence of Language and Secrets of the Arabic*), Beirut: Dar al-Fikr AL-'Arabi.

Totah, K.A. (1926). *The Contribution of the Arabs to Education*. New York: Bureau of Publications, Teachers College, Columbia University.

'Ulwan, A.N. (1994). *Tarbiat al-Awlad fil-Islam* (*Educated Boys in Islam*). Cairo: Dar as-Salam let-Tiba'ah wan Nashr.

'Uthman, Sayyed A. (1989). *At-Ta'allum 'end Burhan al-Islamm az-Zarnooji* (*Learning According to Az-Zarnooji*). Cairo: The Anglo-Egyptian Library.

Von Grunebaum, G.E. (1947). *Instruction of the Student: The Method of Learning.* New York: King's Crown Press.

Von Grunebaum, G.E. (1969). *Islam.* London: Broadway House, Carter Lane.

10

Teaching Aids in Islam

Mujibul Hasan Siddiqui and *Barkat Para*

Introduction

Islam gives such enormous importance to knowledge and education. When the Qur'an began to be revealed, the first word of its first verse was Iqra' which means "read". Thus, education is the preliminary theme of every human development. Education is a light that spectacles the mankind the right direction to flow. If education fails to inculcate self-discipline and commitment to achieve in the minds of student, it is not totally their fault. We as educators play an important role in making the learning process interesting and enjoyable. We have to convert education into a sport and learning process has to generate interest in the students and motivate them to stay back in the institution than to run away from it. Education should become a fun and excitement to them rather than burden and tediousness (Damodharan and Rengarajan, 2007).

Learning is complex phenomenon and needs the immersion of multiple elements and that these elements together occur in the classroom environment is particularly significant and sensitive. The major factors which involved in the learning process in the classroom, including the state of physical, emotional, and personality of the teacher, the content of training, etiquette training, teaching space and teaching aids. Among these factors, as the theory and practice of teaching aids harmonizes special place. Use by the teacher during teaching aids, makes the material presented in cognitive organization fit students and students to achieve significant learning regular and systematic use of teaching aids under each school can be forgotten and often the lack of teaching aids through lack of time and lack the means of justification. The efficient utilization of audio-visual equipment and materials by the classroom teacher requires the acquisition of a new set of skills and understandings.

Meaning of Teaching Aids/ Teaching Learning Material (TLM)

As we all know that today's age is the age of science and technology. The teaching learning programmes have also been affected by it. The process of teaching-learning depends upon the different kind of apparatus available in the classroom. Therefore, for an effective teaching a teacher must need the teaching aid; which works as a supplement along with other teaching methods in class room setting. Teaching aids are tool and equipment used in teaching as an enhancement in class room instruction to enrich the interest of students. Teaching materials are important facilitators of effective instructions. Besides the traditional teaching methods, there are wide varieties of teaching aids available to the teacher. They help students to improve reading and other skill.

In the present age of science and technology, the process of teaching and learning also depends on the latest technology. Teaching becomes interesting when a teacher uses different teaching materials because it directly involves student in the teaching-learning process. It makes lessons enjoyable and memorable. Teaching materials are key factor in creating effective teaching and learning environments. These aids directly address to the five senses so the chances of forgetting become less and process of learning becomes more effective.

In the field of education, TLM is a commonly used acronym that stands for "teaching/learning materials." Broadly, the term refers to a range of educational materials that teachers use in the classroom to support specific learning objectives, as set out in. These can be games, videos, flashcards, project supplies, and more. Classroom teaching that uses only a teacher lecturing the class, perhaps writing on the chalkboard or whiteboard is the classic example of not using any TLM. Activity-based learning employs a variety of teaching/learning materials and focus on student interaction to learn new concepts. Context-specific learning materials enhance the process.

Webster Dictionary defines teaching aid as "an object (such as a book, picture, chart or map) or device (such as a dvd, projector or computer) used by a teacher to enhance or invigorate classroom instruction."

Educational aids improve the efficiency of education in terms of quality and quantity, as well as the objectivity of such equipment is up to the course. (Adgardyl, 1969).

Need and Significance of Teaching Aids

As already mentioned above those teaching aids make the teaching learning process easy and enjoyable; It clears the concepts in an easy and effective manner. Therefore, taking these points into consideration the facts indicate the need and significance of using teaching aids:

(1) Forgetting is the natural phenomenon. Every individual has the tendency to forget. Proper usage of teaching aids helps to retain more concepts permanently.
(2) Students can learn better when they are motivated properly through different teaching aids. There learning will also improve in a positive way.
(3) Teaching aids develop the proper image when the students see, hear, taste and smell properly; or we say the students get first-hand experience through teaching aids.
(4) Teaching aids provide complete example for conceptual thinking.
(5) The teaching aids create the environment of interest for the students.
(6) Teaching aids help to increase the vocabulary of the students.
(7) Teaching aids help the teacher to get some time and make learning permanent.
(8) Teaching aids provide direct experience to the students.
(9) Teaching aids make teaching learning process more interesting and joyful.

Importance of Teaching Aids

Teaching aids play a very vital role in Teaching-Learning process. The following points will highlight the Importance of Teaching aids properly:

(1) Motivation

Motivation is an important factor in learning process. Various theories have been put forth on motivation from time to time by different psychologists. The fact is that when students are motivated to learn something then they can do so otherwise the result will be different. Therefore, we can say that Teaching aids motivate the students so that they can learn better.

(2) Clarification

We know that there are individual differences among students. Even the twins have difference in their personality. It is difficult for a teacher to clarify the concepts in traditional way. When teacher uses teaching aids, he/she can clarify the subject matter more easily.

(3) Discouragement of Cramming

Mostly in lecture method technique what we see there is a cramming of concepts. Teaching aids can facilitate the proper understanding to the students which discourage the act of cramming. Thus, a good teacher uses TLM with traditional ways of methods in order to get more accurate and systematic results.

(4) Increase the Vocabulary

Vocabulary is must for any student. If there is rich vocabulary a student can understand the concepts very easily and he can write any topic on his own viewpoint. Teaching aids help to increase the vocabulary of the students more effectively.

(5) Saves Time and Money

Teaching aids save the time of both the students and teachers. An English idiom clarifies it very accurately that "A picture is worth a thousand words". It refers to the notion that a complex idea can be conveyed with just a single still image or that an image of a subject conveys its meaning or essence more effectively than a description does.

(6) Classroom Live and active

Teaching aids make the classroom live and active. Because all the senses gets influenced by using teaching aid. It also makes students active listeners and two way communication process takes place.

(7) Avoids Dullness

Effective Teaching aids make students motivate and ready to learn; they participate actively in any class room task. Therefore, we can say that teaching aids perish the dullness of students and make them active.

(8) Direct Experience

When teaching aids are used in science classes; the teacher use laboratory resources or field trip. It ensures and provides direct experience to the students which results a meaningful teaching learning process.

Teacher as a Teaching Aid

As we know in the classroom, to make educational atmosphere feasible and perfect, the teacher need to use many teaching aids. Teaching aids is a tool that is used by the teacher to present new language and material in a systematic way. It can also be used to kindle students or relieve anxiety, fears or dullness since many teaching aids are like games. Some of the most common teaching aids include visual aids like the blackboard, pictures; audio aids like cassette tapes or CDs; and audio visual aids such as video tapes and so on, even the teacher are also a source of visual aids. Thus, before going to discuss the types of teaching aids let us have a look on the role of teacher as a teaching aid in the classroom.

- Teacher as a controller: The teacher is in complete responsibility of the class, what students do, what they say and how they say it. The teacher assumes this role when new language is being introduced and accurate reproduction and drilling technique when needed.

- Teacher can be a story teller: Sometimes we can teach our lesson through stories, especially for kids in this regard teacher become a main tool.
- Teacher is the resource: The teacher is a kind of walking resource centre (monitor) ready to offer help if needed or providing students with whatever language they lack when performing communicative activities. The teacher must make her/himself available so that students can consult her/him when (and only when) they wish.
- Teacher is Organizer: Perhaps the most difficult and important role the teacher has to play. The success of many activities depends on good organization and on the students knowing exactly what they are to do. Giving instructions is vital in this role as well as setting up activities.
- Teacher is Participant: This role improves the atmosphere in the class when the teacher takes part in an activity. However, the teacher takes a risk of dominating the activity when performing it.
- Teacher is Tutor: The teacher acts as a coach when students are involved in project work or self-study. The teacher provides advice and guidance and helps students clarify ideas and limit tasks.
- Teacher can be a model: They make example and student follow.
- Teacher is a real object: Teacher can use everything to apply in classroom such as postures, gestures, body languages, eye contact, facial expressions. For example, when they teach the new word "Swimming", they can use body languages to describe this action...

In teaching process, it is important to generate student's interest. If interest is assembled properly, the learning process can take place effectively. For this purpose use of teaching material is vital as they have the potentials to stimulate interest in teaching-learning process. Richard (1981), in his study found that a normal human being remembers 10 per cent of what they read, 50 per cent of what they saw and heard, above 70 per cent of what they heard, seen and done. An old Chinese proverb also explains the same view:

I hear and forget.
I see and remember
I do and I understand.

It seems important that for better teaching process, a teacher should arrange different aids with the help of which he should make learning easy, enjoyable and stable. As Goethe said "knowing is not enough we must apply, willing is not enough we must do." There are many aids available these days.

Audio Visual Aids

Audio visual aids must be grasped in their correlation to teaching as a whole and to the learning process as a whole, until the teacher comprehends the relationship between audio visual material and teaching learning process.

Audio visual materials are created, distributed and used as strategic components of educational programmes. It supports the process of learning that is motivation, classification and stimulation. Audio visual aids are multisensory materials which motivate and kindle the individual. It makes dynamic learning experience more concrete, realistic and transparent. It provides significant gains in thinking and reasoning.

Audio visual aids are sensitive tools used in teaching and as paths for learning. These are planned educational materials that appeal to the senses of the people and quicken learning facilities for clear understanding. Senses have been given utmost importance in Islam for example there are lot of verses on "Tadabur", "Tafakur", "Sama", "Basar", "aqal", etc. which shows that senses are used while examining any reality. Heart is also a great source of understanding in Islamic teaching. Thus, apart in gaining knowledge we use these gifts which God bestowed us. Let's clear the meaning and importance of audio visual aids in the light of few definitions below:

1. ***According to Kinder S. James***: Audio visual aids are any device which can be used to make the learning experience more concrete, more realistic and more dynamic.

2. ***According to Burton***: Audio visual aids are those sensory objects or images which initiate or stimulate and reinforce learning.

3. ***According to Carter V. Good:*** Audio visual aids are those aids which help in completing the triangular process of learning that is motivation, classification and stimulation.

4. ***According to Good's Dictionary of Education***: Audio visual aids are anything by means of which learning process may be encouraged or carried on through the sense of hearing or sense of sight.

5. ***According to Edger Dale:*** Audio visual aids are those devices by the use of which communication of ideas between persons and groups in various teaching and training situations is helped. These are also termed as multi-sensory materials.

Purposes

- To supplement and enrich teachers particular teaching to make teaching-learning more concrete and enjoyable.
- To assist an instructional role in itself.
- To generate interest among the group.
- To make teaching as an effective process.

Advantages

1. Audio visual Aids help in effective perceptual and conceptual learning.
2. Audio visual Aids are helpful in capturing and sustaining attention of students.
3. Audio visual Aids arouse interest and motivate students to learn.
4. Audio visual Aids are helpful in new learning.
5. Audio visual Aids help in saving energy and time of both the teachers and students.
6. Audio visual Aids provide near realistic experience.
7. Audio visual Aids can meet individual demands.
8. Audio visual Aids are useful for mass education.

Characteristics of good teaching aids

Some characteristics of good Teaching aids are given below:

1. Good teaching aids are always meaningful and purposeful.

2. Good teaching aids aim to motivate the learners.
3. Good teaching aids are always accurate in every aspect.
4. Good teaching aids should be simple and cheap.
5. There is always an opportunity of Improvisation in good teaching aids.
6. Mostly the teaching aids should be Large in size.
7. Good teaching aids must be Up-to-date and easily portable.

Principles to be Followed for the Effective Use of Audio Visual Aids

- In any educational programme audio visual aids must function as a central part.
- In educational programmes audio visual aids should be centralized, under specialized direction and leadership.
- To assist in selection and coordination of audio visual materials an advisory committee consisting of representative from all areas of curriculum should be appointed.
- An educational programme should be flexible.
- In order to eliminate duplication, easy accessibility and convenient use audio visual material should be carefully located.
- Audio visual material should be available whenever and wherever they needed for effective utilization as an integral part of curriculum.
- Budget appropriations should be made regularly for audio visual education programmes.
- Periodic evaluation to be done to assess the function of, utilization and expenditure of the programme.

Classification of Audio Visual Aids

We may classify these aids as follows:

Visual Aids
Audio Aids
Audio-Visual Aids

(1) Visual Aids

The aids which use senses of vision are called Visual aids. For example: actual objects, models, pictures, charts, maps, flash cards, flannel board, bulletin board, chalkboard, overhead projector, slides etc. Out of these black board and chalk are the commonest ones. Here is the explanation of some of the visual aids:

Graphic Aids

It is an amalgamation of graphic and pictorial material designed for the orderly and logical visualizing of relationships between key facts and ideas for example: comparisons, relative amounts developments, processes, classification or organization. It is a visual art based upon symbolic and abstract forms, it is somewhat less abstract than words, numbers and formulas, but more abstract than pictorial displays are. There are several kinds of graphic presentations: charts, maps, diagrams, graphs, and cartoons. Following are the illustration of some of these graphic aids:

Graphs

Graphs depict numerical or qualitative relationships. The graphs are of two types– statistical and mathematical. Statistical graphs portray data by lengths of bars, lengths and slopes of lines, by areas, by volumes and countable units. They are not only effective tools for condensing, relating and communicating data, but they are also designed and prepared for efficient and realistic recording and analysis. On the other hand, mathematical graph pictures a function in order to reveal the relationship between variables, to assist in the solution of an equation, or to speed a computation.

Charts

These visual symbols are used for summarizing, comparing, contrasting or performing other services in explaining subject matter. A chart is a combination of pictorial, graphic, numerical or vertical material, which presents a clear summary. Chart is defined as a visual aid which portrays pictorial and written key information in systematic way to summarize, compare, for example: anatomical charts and figure, diagrams etc.

Chart showing the organization and development of a process can take various forms. The tree chart presents material symbolized by roots, trunk, branches and leaves. Flow charts are systematic arrangements showing trend, movements and organization. The stream chart indicates how several different factors can be brought together to form a larger event. Time charts are used to indicate the chronology of a series of events or to arrange chronologically those happenings important to the development of a process, a company or a nation. Issue charts are especially helpful in highlighting the contrasting views of individuals or organizations on pertinent topics. Pictorial charts make use of conventional or symbolic illustrations of topics that are being treated: e.g., automobiles, factories, population growth etc. in teaching Islamic studies charts play a vital role in order to get familiar with the historical events of Islam, the charts help us to demonstrate these events and happening in a systematic way.

Purposes

- To visualize an item, it is otherwise difficult to explain only in words.
- To highlight important points.
- To provide outline for materials covered in presentation.
- To show continuity in process.
- For creating problems and stimulating thinking.
- For showing development of structure.

Maps

A map is a symbolic depiction emphasizing relationships between elements of some space, such as objects, regions, or themes. Webster defines a map as, "A representation (usually on a flat surface) of the surface of the earth or some part of it, showing relative size and position, according to scale or projection of position represented." Maps are graphic representations of the earth's surface, or portions of it. Map reading and map drawing are important skills to learn in geography. Maps use symbols like lines and different colours to show features such as rivers, roads, cities or mountains. Young geographers need to be able to understand symbols. All these symbols help us to visualize what things on the ground actually look like.

Maps also help us to identify distances so that we know how far away one thing is from another. We need to be capable to estimate distances on maps because all maps show the earth or regions within it as a much smaller size than their real size. To do this we need to be able to read the scale on a map. Thus, in teaching of Islam, maps are rich source to get acquainted with Islamic geography and all about that.

Diagrams

Diagrams are visual descriptions that explain rather than represent. The symbolism in many cases is quite abstract and requires understanding and study on the part of the student for proper interpretation of the material. Diagrams of electrical circuits, data radii of circles, etc., impart a form or unity to an object or process that exists only in the abstract. Diagrams should be used with care only in those instances herein students have demonstrated a capability for comprehending such abstraction.

Flash Cards

"Flash cards are a set of pictured paper cards of varying sizes that are flashed one by one in a logical sequence." Flash cards can be self-made or commercially prepared and are made up of chart or drawing paper, plain paper using colours or ink on them for drawings.

Purposes:

1. To teach the students.
2. To give health education.
3. Useful for small group.
4. Used in group discussions.

Using the flashcards

For class room instruction, the flash card is to be properly used. The following steps are used while displaying flash cards.

1. Give brief introduction about the lesson to students.
2. Give instructions to students about their actions while you flash the cards.
3. Flash the card in front of the class by holding it high with both your hands so that all the students can see it.
4. Let the student respond as per instructions already given.
5. Review the lesson by selectively using flash cards.

Advantages

- Flash cards can be used to introduce and present topics.
- It can be used to apply information already gained by students to new situations
- It can be used to review a topic.
- Can be used for drill and practice in elementary classes.
- To develop the cognitive abilities of recognition and recall of students.
- It can work as a useful supplementary aid and can be effectively used with other material.

Disadvantages

- Cannot be used for a large group.
- Prone to get spoiled soon.
- Preparation is time consuming.

Posters

"Posters are the graphic aids with short, quick and typical messages with attention capturing paintings."

Purposes

- To provide general motivation.
- To create an aesthetic or atmospheric effect.
- To communicate a more general idea.
- For the class room and community.

Preparation and Rules

- To do a special job.

- To promote one point.
- To support local demonstration.
- Planned for specified people
- Tell the message at single glance.
- Use bold letters.
- Use pleasing colours.
- It should be placed where people pass or gather.

Features of a Good Poster

- Brevity: message should be concise.
- Simplicity: message should be easily understandable.
- Idea: should base on single idea and it should be relevant.
- Colour: suitable colour and combination should be used to make the poster attractive and eye catching.
- Display: while displaying one should be sure to find a place where there is adequate light and where the larger population will see it.

Advantages

- It attracts attention.
- It conveys the message very quickly.
- It does not require a detailed study.
- Good poster leads to action with good motivation.
- It can stand alone and is self-explanatory.

Disadvantages

Poster does not always give enough information when a poster is seen for longer time it may not attractive. So it should be dynamic.

Blackboard

A blackboard (also known as a chalkboard) is a reusable writing surface on which text or drawings are made with sticks of calcium sulfate or calcium carbonate, known, when used for this purpose, as chalk. Blackboards are originally made of smooth, thin sheets of black or dark grey slate stone. Teachers use it for at least five general purposes, and there are probably others worth exploring.

1. For writing assignments, spelling lists, definitions and other materials, the blackboard are universally used.
2. Visual symbols of all kinds. Teachers draw diagrams to show the subject, verb, and modifiers in a sentence; to work out an example in plane geometry; to represent a cross section of a tree etc.
3. Quite as naturally, they turn the blackboard over to students for activities too familiar to need listing here.
4. Frequently they fill in certain permanent outlines painted on the blackboard, such as outline maps, tabular charts, or other special materials—such as music stuffs, book keeping forms, pupil progress charts.
5. Less frequently a teacher uses the blackboard to give a "chalk talk", that is, a lecture accompanied with simple drawing to make graphic some particular ideas.

Bulletin Boards

The bulletin board, as its name suggests, should be a place for the posting of "bulletin"—timely, brief items that are "news" to the students. The news may be announcement of a meeting, a photograph, a clipping, a book jacket, etc., it must be newsworthy and attractive. There are several kinds of bulletin boards. Quite commonly we cover wall space with some kind of durable cloth. Items can be tacked onto it. Or the bulletin board may be portable, made from press board, plywood, basswood, heavy linoleum, or something similar. It might be hinged on sides and folded; it might be suspended from to eyes on hooks so that it can be taken down when necessary. Thus, in a nutshell we can say that bulletin boards are very effective aids in teaching of any kind of subject; because it familiars us about the main motive of any kind news etc.

Bulletin boards are used not only by a single classroom, but often by grades, by departments, or by the entire school. Different materials apply to each, but the principles are the same. The board must be ill-lit, properly placed in the flow of traffic, attractive, and readable and it must be related to pupil activity. One method of assuring variety and interest is the "morgue" principle followed by newspapers. This is the collection of material filed for future use but accumulated continuously. We can include not merely items for future display but sketches or reproductions of particularly effective bulletin boards observed, and adaptable to your own needs.

(2) Audio Aids

The aids that involve the sense of hearing are called Audio aids. For example: radio, tape recorder, gramophone etc. Here is the explanation of some of the audio aids:

Radio

Radio has long held out promise of being of invaluable assistance to the teacher in the classroom because it is a means of presenting worthwhile learning experiences simultaneously to large numbers of students. In remote areas, it is particularly helpful in competently covering subject matter that might otherwise not be offered at all. It is an important and easily accessible audio aid serving three important purposes "news, views and recreation".

Usefulness of Radio in Classroom

1. It is a powerful means of developing listening comprehension.
2. It can also help the pupils to acquire correct pronunciation and phonetics like tape recorders.
3. Conversational style and language can be learned on the radio.
4. Mass education goals can be achieved through radio broadcast.
5. The lectures of the eminent persons like scientists, educationists, historians and other professionals can be broadcast on the radio.
6. The effectiveness of the radio programmes and the lessons is also increased by the introduction of sound effect of rain, thunder, waterfall, chirping of birds and background noises.
7. News listened on the radio can improve our general knowledge.
8. It improves the word power of learners.

Tape Recorder and Audio Cassettes

Cassette type audio tapes are available now which can play for 90 minutes on both the sides. We listen to our own recorded voice, recorded speeches of politicians and learned people, recorded poem of great composers, songs, music etc. by the tape recorder. It is an effective audio aid used in classroom for active learning.

Implementation of Tape Recorder in the Classroom

In classroom tape recorder helps the students to overcome poor speech habits such as faulty pronunciation, poor choice of words, grammatical errors, speaking too rapidly or too slowly, "bunching" word, and poor inflection or accent. It can be used to record sample of individual student performance for purpose of self-evaluation. The tape records helps students correct actual speech defects such as nasal resonance, slurring of syllables, giving incorrect vowel values, lisping too much force to sibilants, and stammering. In a nutshell we can say that use of tape recorder in the classroom helps train students to express ideas clearly, concisely, logically, and forcefully.

(3) Audio-Visual Aids

The aids which involve the sense of vision as well as hearing are called Audio-visual aids. For example: television, film projector, film strips etc.

(i) Television

TV differs from radio in the sense that it is audio and visual both. We can see the incident occurring round the globe on it immediately after the occurrence of the incident through telecast. Thus, it is bi-sensory (multisensory) media. We get news, views and recreation through television in the same way as we do through the transistor but in more compact and concrete way due to facility of vision here.

Advantages of Television

I. It heightens the reality more than the physical presence.

II. It can overcome the barriers of time and space.
III. TV experiences are new and versatile. So, they can bring variety to classroom teaching by breaking monotony and strengthening the learning structures by its multisensory approach.
IV. It widens the horizon of pupils' experiences by giving them up to date knowledge of the real situation and by making them conversant with the opinions of others.
V. It motives the students for learning by arousing and relating their interest in the leaning situation.

Limitations of Television

i. Speed of television cannot be changed as we can do in motion pictures.
ii. A TV programme cannot be adjusted to teaching and *vice versa* will have to done. A teacher can take the help of video recording in such cases.

Overhead Projector

The overhead projector is the most used in all audio visual aids. It projects transparencies with brilliant screen images appropriate for use in a lighted room. The teacher can write or draw diagrams on the transparency while he teaches; these are projected simultaneously on the screen by the OHP.

During Presentation

- Keep the screen above the heads of the participants.
- Keep the screen in full view of participants.
- Make sure you are not blocking anyone's view when presenting.
- Darken the room appropriately by blocking out sunshine and dimming nearby.
- Turn the screen off between slides if you are going to talk for more than two.
- Talk to the audience, not to the screen.

Purposes

- To develop concepts and sequences in a subject matter area in a systematic way.
- To make peripheral notes on the transparencies for the use of the teacher that can carry without divulging them to the class.
- To test students' performances, while other classmates observe.
- To show relationships by means of transparent overlays in contrasting colour.
- To give the illusion of motion in the transparency.

Advantages

- It permits the teacher to stand in front of the class while using the projector, thus enabling her to point out features appearing on the screen by pointing to the materials at the projector itself and at the same time, to observe the students' reactions to her discussion.
- Gains attention of the student.

Overhead Transparencies

Transparencies are popular instructional medium. They are simple to formulate, easy to prepare and easy to operate with the overhead projector which is light weight.

A 10 ×10 inches sheet with printed, written or drawn material is placed on the platform of the projector and a large image is projected on a screen behind you.

The projector is used from near to the front of the room with the teacher standing or sitting beside, facing the student.

Guidelines for making effective transparencies:

- Each transparency should contain one main idea.
- Only related figures and diagrams should be included.
- In writing simple lettering style must be used.
- Use diagrams in proposition to its lettering.
- Keep the message clear and simple.

- The key messages should be emphasized here.
- Use colour and lettering with discretion.

Advantages

- It permits face to face interaction with the students.
- It can be used in daylight conditions.
- It can present information in systemic developmental sequences.
- It requires limited planning and can be prepared in variety of inexpensive methods.
- It is easily available.

The Opaque Projector

Opaque projector is the only projector on which you can project a multiplicity of materials for example: book pages, objects, coins, postcards, or any other similar flat material that is non-transparent.

The opaque projector will project and simultaneously enlarge, directly from the originals, printed matter, all kinds of written or pictorial matter in any sequence derived by the teacher. It requires a dark room, as projector is large and not reality movables.

Advantages

- It stimulates attention and arouses interest among students.
- We can project a wide range of materials like stamps, coins, specimen, when one copy is available.
- It can be used for enlarging drawings, pictures and maps.
- Does not require any written or typed materials; hand-written material can be used.
- It helps students to retain knowledge for longer period.
- Review instructional problems.
- Test knowledge and ability.
- Simple operation.

Disadvantages

- Costly equipment.
- Needs to use it with care.
- Needs a dark room for projection.

Slide Projector

A slide is a small piece of transparent material on which a single pictorial image or scene or graphic image has been photographed or reproduced otherwise. Simple 'Slide projector' was known as "magic lantern" in the olden days. The principle here is that when we put the transparent slide on the socket and throw light from behind, the light passes through it and projects the image on the screen.

Slides are a form of projected media that are easy to prepare. They are still pictures on positive film which you can process and mount individually yourself or send to a film laboratory. The standard size of the slides is 2" × 2". Any 35mm camera will make satisfactory slides.

Types of Slides

1. **Photographic slides:** 2" × 2" 3" × 4"
   (a) Black and white
   (b) Coloured
2. **Handmade slides:** can be made with
   (a) Acetate sheet
   (b) Cellophane
   (c) Etched glass
   (d) Plain glass

Slides can be prepared from photographs and pictures by teachers and pupils taking photographs and snapshots when they go on fieldtrips for historical, geographical, literacy or scientific excursions. The arrangement of slides in proper sequence, according to the topic discussed, is an important aspect of teaching with them.

Advantages

1. Requires only filming, processing and mounting by self or laboratory.
2. Results in colourful, realistic, reproduction original subject.
3. Preparation with any 35mm camera for most uses.
4. Easy to revise and up-date.

5. Easily handled, stored and re-arranged for various uses.
6. Can be combined with tape narration or can control time for discussion.
7. May be adapted to group or individual use.

Filmstrips

Film strips are series of transparent still pictures with distinct frames on 35mm film. A tap recorded narration can be harmonized with film strip. Each strip contains from 12 to 18 or more pictures. It is a fixed sequence of related stills on a roll of 35mm film or 8mm film. Film strips are used before a large group of students either for introducing a lesson or for elaborating some minute object not seen in ordinary situations.

Principles

1. Preview filmstrips before using them and selected carefully to meet the needs of the topic to be taught.
2. Show again any part of the filmstrip needing more specific study.
3. Use filmstrip to stimulate emotions, build attitudes and to point up problems.
4. It should be introduced appropriately and its relationship to the topic of the study brought out.
5. Use a pointer to direct attention, to specific details on the screen.

Types of Filmstrip

1. **Discussion filmstrip**: It is continuous strip of film consisting of individual frames arranged in sequence usually with explanatory titles.
2. **Sound slide film**: It is similar to filmstrip but instead of explanatory titles or spoken discussion recorded explanation is audible, which is synchronized with the pictures.

Advantages of Film Strips

1. Filmstrips are compact, easily handled and always in proper sequence.

2. They can be supplemented with recordings.
3. They are inexpensive when quantity reproduction is required.
4. They are useful for group or individual study at projection rate is controlled by instructor or user.
5. They are projected with simple light weight equipment.

Limitations of Film Strips

1. Because of limited focal length they can be used only in small sized classes.
2. Fixed order of the film strips creates problem in handling individual frames.
3. Many schools do not have audio visual workshops and thus, they depend on the cheap and unstandardized materials available in the market.

Computers

It is the latest electronic device with audio and visual both. It accepts data, performs operations on that data in sequence (decided by a programme) and outputs the results. From input devices to output devices computers have a wide range of applicability in education. In computers inputs are converted into output by a programme. Thus input (data) plus programme form software or instructional programme. Inputs are converted into output in the CPU of the computer.

Computers always work according to the programme given to it. Whatever instruction or programme, the student gives to computers, it will always act accordingly and output will also come out on the same line. Application of computers in education can be understood by the following lines.

Application of Computers in Instructional Situation

1. Pre-testing of student's knowledge for admission.
2. Planning and printing individualized programmes like CAI, CAL etc.
3. Monitoring student's progress.
4. Compiling tests for evaluation.

5. Scoring of the test items.
6. Storing data files and information for future use.
7. Using internet for distance learning.

Advantage of Computers for Learners

Gaining knowledge through computer is a new experience for learners. They can be benefited from computers in the following ways:

1. Computers motivate the students to deal with complex situations and reinforce them. Thus, we see a direct interaction between a student and the computer.
2. Learning process becomes individualized and flexible through computers. It means that every student gets chance to learn according to his own ability.
3. Students can increase their educational achievement through computers.
4. Computer develops the critical thinking power of students. When a students progresses on computer programme, he is compelled to think why it is happening so.
5. Computer provides them chance how to progress on an instructional programme by avoiding mistakes. As soon as student commits a mistake, he is immediately instructed by the computer what mistake he had done and how can it be removed.

Conclusion

Teaching aid or TLM is a best tool in the hands of a teacher to foster the learning among children. The difficult and hard concepts are presented in such manner through teaching aids that students are able to learn easily and in feasible way. That is why nowadays most of the teachers use a wide range of TLM in classroom setting. If we look in the Islamic point of view, it gives us clear idea that there are number of teaching learning material which help us to propagate or enhance learning. The Holy Qur'an has emphasized three subjects more precisely and dominantly such as Nature, Human Conscience and History. In nature, it is clearly said about sky, stars, universe, galaxies, so on so forth which means all the basic science such as physics, chemistry, astronomy, and biology etc. are coming in this part of subject. And the teaching learning material such as charts, pc's, projectors, power point presentation, field trip, firsthand experience, laboratory, library etc. will be used for an effective explanation of such concepts.

In human conscience the nature of man, his relationship with God and other people, with society etc. comes which reflects the finest creation of God. Introspection, observation and so and so forth will be used as a method of studying behaviour. When it comes to teaching history there are lot of methods and aids which can be used to simplify the concepts of history such as role model, globe, maps, manuscripts, etc. In Islam, history has been given an abundant importance; because it aware us about the positives and negatives of our past. When we read history its present facts and past experiences save us for indulging in waste activities or in any such kind of action. It also aware us about the mistakes or privileges of our forefathers; which enables us to take a lesson from their deeds either in positive way or in negatives. Thus, for understanding any concept, its clarification is mandatory which is the base of any notion.

At last we can say that Teaching aids are an integral part in the teaching-learning process. They are determined by the other lesson components and the learning conditions. Teaching aids have a abundant role to play in the communicative approach since they help learning in a number of different ways: They can revitalize up the classroom and bring more assortment and interest into language lessons. They can help to provide the situations (contexts) which light up the meaning of the expressions used. They can inspire students to speak the language as well as to read it and write it. They can help in generous information of one kind or another about the background of literature and about life in the foreign country concerned.

REFERENCES

Ahmad, Z.A. *et.al*, (2006). *Study Guide for Islamic Studies*. Petaling Jaya: Prentice Hall Pearson Malaysia Sdn. Bhd.

Ansari, M.S. (2014). *Education*. Paper-II and III. New Delhi: Ramesh Publishing House.

Dale, E. (1948). *Audio-Visual Methods in Teaching*. New York. The Dryden Press.

Douglas, H. (2000). *Teaching by Principles: An Interactive Approach to Language Pedagogy*. Prentice Hall Regents Englewood Cliffs, New Jersey 07632.

Wan Noor Hazlina and Kamaruzaman Jusof (2009). "Using multimedia in teaching Islamic studies." *Journal of Media and Communication Studies*, Vol. 1(5) pp. 086-094, Terengganu, Malaysia.

Pula, F.R. ((1968). *Application and Operation of Audiovisual Equipment in Education*. USA

https://www.thoughtco.com/tlm-teaching-learning-materials-2081658

https://www.merriamwebster.com/dictionary/teaching%20aid

http://www.askaboutireland.ie/learning-zone/primary-students/5th-+-6th-class/geography/maps-and-map-reading/what-are-maps/why-use-maps/ 13/02/18

https://peltjournal.wordpress.com/2013/09/30/the-most-important-teaching-aids-in-the-classroom-the-teacher-and-the-blackboard-ha-thi-huong/

http://www.publishyourarticles.net/knowledge-hub/education/what-is-the-importance-of-teaching-aids-in-learning/5277/

http://www.ehow.com/list_6100903_types-teaching-aids.html

11
Evaluation in Teachings of Islam

Kounsar Jabeen

1.1 Introduction

The discussion of evaluation of Islamic education learning is associated to how much the instructional material is ultimately internalized by the students which, at a later turn, is expressed in the students' daily behaviours. Thus far, learning outcomes have been seen as scores obtained from tests or examinations. The affective and psycho-motoric learning aspects have not been popular among teachers, including Islamic education teachers. Evaluation of Islamic education learning outcome should be comprehensive casing the aspects of knowledge, skills, and attitudes. A need thus arises to expand an Islamic education learning evaluation model that is all-inclusive.

Islamic education has a basic structure of thoughts that becomes an indication for all educational practices in all aspects of human life. The basic thought frame is constructed of the three basic concepts of faith, devotion, and good deeds. These basic concepts form the hub of Islamic teachings that must be adopted as the foundation structure of every system. These three basic teachings have been developed by clerics into three concept studies of faith related to matters of belief in God, laws related to matters of behaviours, and good deeds related to goods behaviours.

The three basic concepts are concerned with synergic and harmonious dealings to produce compatibility, harmony, and balance in the four relation kinds. The first is the relation between man and his Creator in terms of how far humans have fulfilled their responsibilities to the Creator. The second is the relation among humans in which no one is to act in such a way that it will hurt others. The third is the relation between humans and animals and environment in which no one is to impact destruction. The fourth is the relation between man and himself, in which humans must behave themselves.

1.2 Meaning of Evaluation

Evaluation is an organized determination of a subject's merit, value and significance, using criteria governed by a set of standards. It can assist an organization, programme, project or any other intervention or initiative to gauge any aim, realisable concept/proposal, or any alternative, to help in decision-making; or to determine the degree of achievement or value in regard to the aim and objectives and results of any such deed that has been finished. The main purpose of evaluation, in addition to acquisition of insight into prior or existing initiatives, is to enable reflection and support in the identification of future change. Evaluation is often used to portray and assess subjects of interest in a wide range of human enterprises, including the arts, criminal, foundations, non-profit organizations, government, health care, and other human services. It is long term and done at the end of a period of time.

The term of evaluation comes from English language "evaluation", means valuation and assessment. The evaluation term is newly on education. Rice, a founder of evaluation activities from United States of America, did not use evaluation term yet; even his work is an evaluation work. Tyler use evaluation term on his book entitled: *Basic Principles of Curriculum and Instruction* written in 1949. Tyler (1932) as cited by Guba (1982) define the evaluation as an empirical data comparison process of academics performance and have an explicit purpose to determine how that purpose is realized. Morrison as Oemar Hamalik (1990 page 2) cite, said that evaluation as a consideration base on a set criteria agreement and accountably. So that, there are three main evaluation factors as Morison said, they are (1) judgment, (2) assessment object description, and (3) accountability criteria.

Evaluation is the planned explanation and giving of meaning to predicted or actual impacts of proposals or results. It looks at original objectives, and at what is either predicted or what was accomplished and how it was accomplished. So evaluation can be formative that is taking place during the development of a concept or proposal, project or organization, with the intention of improving the value or effectiveness of the proposal, project, or organisation. It can also be summative drawing lessons from a completed action or project or an organisation at a later point in time or circumstance.

Evaluation is inherently a notionally informed approach (whether explicitly or not), and consequently any particular definition of evaluation would have been personalized to its context – the theory, needs, purpose, and methodology of the evaluation process itself. Having said this, evaluation has been defined as:

- A systematic, rigorous, and meticulous application of scientific methods to assess the design, implementation, improvement, or outcomes of a programme. It is a resource-intensive process, frequently requiring resources, such as, evaluates expertise, labour, time, and a sizable budget.
- "The critical assessment, is an objective manner as possible, of the degree to which a service or its component parts fulfils stated goals" (St Leger and Wordsworth-Bell).
- "A study designed to assist some audience to assess an object's merit and worth" (Stufflebeam).

1.3 Purpose of Evaluation

The main purpose of a programme evaluation can be to "determine the quality of a programme by formulating a judgment", Marthe Hurteau, Sylvain Houle, Stéphanie Mongiat (2009).

An alternative view is that "projects, evaluators, and other stakeholders (including funders) will all have potentially diverse ideas about how best to evaluate a project since each may have a different definition of 'merit'. The interior of the problem is thus about defining what is of value." From this perspective, evaluation "is a contested term", as "evaluators" use the term evaluation to describe an assessment, or enquiry of a programme whilst others simply comprehend evaluation as being synonymous with applied research.

There are two functions considering to the evaluation purpose. Formative Evaluations provide the information on the improving a product or a process. Summative Evaluations provide information of short-term efficiency or long-term impact to deciding the espousal of a product or process. Not all evaluations serve the similar purpose, some evaluations serve a monitoring function rather than focusing solely on measurable programme outcomes or evaluation findings and a full list of types of evaluations would be difficult to compile. This is because evaluation is not part of an integrated theoretical framework, drawing on a number of disciplines, which include management and organisational theory, policy analysis, education, sociology, social anthropology, and social change.

1.4 Methods of Evaluation

In the process of evaluation we can use quantitative and qualitative data, or often utilize both. Both methods afford vital information for evaluation, and both can improve community engagement and education system in a systematic manner. These methods are rarely used alone; combined, they generally provide the best overview of the project. Broadly there are two methods involving in the process of evaluation. These are:

1.4.1 Quantitative Methods

Quantitative data provide information that can be counted to answer such questions as "How many?", "Who was involved?", "What were the outcomes?", and "How much did it cost?" Quantitative data can be collected by surveys or questionnaires, pre-tests and post-tests, observation, or review of existing documents and databases or by gathering clinical data. Surveys may be self- or interviewer-administered and conducted face-to-face or by telephone, by mail, or online. Analysis of quantitative data involves statistical analysis, from basic descriptive statistics to complex analyses.

Quantitative data assess the depth and breadth of an implementation (e.g., the number of people who participated, the number of people who completed the programme). Quantitative data collected before and after an intervention can show its outcomes and impact. The strengths of quantitative data for evaluation purposes include their generalizability (if the sample represents the population), the ease of analysis, and their consistency and precision (if collected reliably). The limits of using quantitative data for evaluation can include poor response rates from surveys, difficulty obtaining documents, and difficulties in valid measurement. In addition, quantitative data do not offer an understanding of the programme's context and may not be vigorous enough to explain complex issues or interactions (Holland, *et al.*, 2005; Garbarino, *et al.*, 2009).

1.4.2 Qualitative Methods

Qualitative data answer such questions as "What is the value added?", "Who was responsible?", and "When did something happen?'' Qualitative data are collected through direct or participant observation, interviews, focus groups, and case studies and from written documents. Analyses of qualitative data include examining, comparing and contrasting, and interpreting patterns. Analysis will likely include the identification of themes, coding, clustering similar data, and reducing data to meaningful and important points, such as in grounded theory-building or other approaches to qualitative analysis (Patton, 2002).

Observations may help enlighten behaviours as well as social context and meanings because the evaluator sees what is actually happening. Observations can include inspection a participant or programme, videotaping an intervention, or even recording people who have been asked to "think aloud" while they work (Ericsson *et al.*, 1993).

Interviews may be conducted with individuals alone or with groups of people and are especially useful for exploring multifarious issues. Interviews may be structured and conducted under controlled conditions, or they may be conducted with a loose set of questions asked in an open-ended manner. It may be helpful to tape-record interviews, with appropriate permissions, to facilitate the analysis of themes or content. Some interviews have a specific focus, such as a critical incident that an individual recalls and describes in detail. Another type of interview focuses on a person's perceptions and motivations.

Focus groups are run by a facilitator who leads a discussion among a group of people who have been chosen because they have specific characteristics (e.g., were clients of the programme being evaluated). Focus group participants discuss their ideas and insights in response to open-ended questions from the facilitator. The strength of this method is that group discussion can provide ideas and stimulate memories with topics cascading as discussion occurs (Krueger *et al.,* 2000; Morgan, 1997).

The strengths of qualitative data contain providing contextual data to clarify complex issues and complementing quantitative data by explaining the "why" and "how" behind the "what." The boundaries of qualitative data for evaluation may include lack of generalizability, the time-consuming and expensive nature of data collection, and the obscurity and difficulty of data analysis and interpretation (Patton, 2002).

1.4.3 Mixed Methods

The evaluation of community engagement and education system may need both qualitative and quantitative methods because of the diversity of issues addressed (e.g., population, type of project, and goals). The choice of methods should fit the need for the evaluation, its timeline, and available resources (Holland *et al.*, 2005; Steckler *et al.*, 1992).

1.5 Types of Evaluation

Since evaluation is a central component of the educative process, the teacher should direct every learning experience in relation to the needs and interest of the learners. Evaluation forms the basis for deciding what type of appraisal is needed to assess a particular learning situation. There are mainly two types of evaluation which are as under:

1.5.1 Formative Evaluation

This type of evaluation the teacher performs the learning activities to find out how well he is doing and what is needed during the next learning experience by the learners. This is important to give the learners adequate information for self-appraisal. This is one way of motivating them. Information from formative evaluation is not used to make decisions or judgments about the learners' work; but rather used on matters as learner's grouping, preparation of lesson plans and execution of teaching strategy.

Formative evaluation is used prior to programme design or implementation. It generates data on the need for the programme and develops the baseline for subsequent monitoring. It also identifies areas of improvement and can furnish insights on what the programme's priorities should be. This helps project managers establish their areas of concern and focus, and increases understanding of your programme in the midst of the target population prior to launch.

When:

New programme development

Programme expansion

What:

The need for your project among the potential beneficiaries

The current baseline of relevant indicators, which can help show impact later

Why:

Helps make early improvements to the programme

Allows project managers to refine or improve the programme

How:

Conduct sample surveys and focus group discussions among the target population focused on whether they are likely to need, understand, and accept programme elements.

Questions to ask:

Is there a need for the programme?

What you can do to improve it?

1.5.2 Summative Evaluation

Under this type, the teacher undertakes the evaluation of the learning outcomes of a unit in order to grade the learners and make his own personal judgment on the effectiveness of his methods of teaching. This evaluation process serves as a basis for deciding whether promotion or retention will be better for the learner. Besides, it can also serve as a guide in determining the effectiveness of instruction and be a gauge for planning future learning activities. Summative evaluations are those used by the teacher to determine grades and form the reports sent to the students and their parents. Evaluating instructional outcomes is compulsory to sustain the approved performance standard of the learners, serves as guide in determining on-going experiences and when to introduce new ones; to appraise the teacher's performance; effectiveness of teaching methodology; availability and suitability of textbook and other printed learning materials; and to identify and measure special abilities of learners.

Summative evaluation is conducted after the programme's completion or at the conclusion of a programme cycle. It generates facts about how well the project delivered benefits to the target population. It is useful for programme administrators to justify the project, show what they have achieved, and lobby for project continuation or expansion.

When:

At the end of a programme

At the end of a programme cycle

What:

How effectively the programme made the desired change happen

How the programme changed the lives of programme participants

Why:

Provides data to justify continuing the programme

Generates insights into the effectiveness and efficiency of the programme

How:

Conduct a review of internal reports and a survey for programme managers and target populations. The aim should be to measure the change that the project has brought about and compare the change to the costs.

Questions to ask:

Should the programme continue to be funded?

Should the programme be expanded? If so, where? What factors worked in its favour and what worked against it?

1.5.3 Diagnostic Evaluation

This is the type of evaluation the teacher considers at the beginning of the unit or course to determine the different levels in terms of learning experience of children to serve as basis for grouping them– slow, average or fast. Diagnostic evaluation will also enable the teacher to ascertain or analyze the nature or cause of difficulties, and, in effect, help them plan remedial activities to meet their interests and needs.

1.6 Approaches of Evaluation

There exist several conceptually distinct ways of thinking about, designing, and conducting evaluation efforts. Many of the evaluation approaches in use today make truly unique contributions to solving important problems, while others refine existing approaches in some way.

1.6.1 Classification of Approaches

Summary of approaches for conducting evaluations				
Approach	**Attribute**			
	Organizer	**Purpose**	**Key strengths**	**Key weaknesses**
Politically controlled	Threats	Get, keep or increase influence, power or money.	Secure evidence advantageous to the client in a conflict.	Violates the principle of full & frank disclosure.
Public relations	Propaganda needs	Create positive public image.	Secure evidence most likely to bolster public support.	Violates the principles of balanced reporting, justified conclusions, & objectivity.
Experimental research	Causal relationships	Determine causal relationships between variables.	Strongest paradigm for determining causal relationships.	Requires controlled setting, limits range of evidence, focuses primarily on results.
Management information systems	Scientific efficiency	Continuously supply evidence needed to fund,	Gives managers detailed	Human service variables are rarely amenable

		direct, & control programmes.	evidence about complex programmes.	to the narrow, quantitative definitions needed.
Testing programmes	Individual differences	Compare test scores of individuals & groups to selected norms.	Produces valid & reliable evidence in many performance areas. Very familiar to public.	Data usually only on testee performance, overemphasizes test-taking skills, can be poor sample of what is taught or expected.
Objectives-based	Objectives	Relates outcomes to objectives.	Common sense appeal, widely used, uses behavioural objectives & testing technologies.	Leads to terminal evidence often too narrow to provide basis for judging the value of a programme.
Content Analysis	Content of a communication	Describe & draw conclusion about a communication.	Allows for unobtrusive analysis of large volumes of unstructured, symbolic materials.	Sample may be unrepresentative yet overwhelming in volume. Analysis design often overly simplistic for question.
Accountability	Performance expectations	Provide constituents with an accurate accounting of results.	Popular with constituents. Aimed at improving quality of products and services.	Creates unrest between practitioners & consumers. Politics often forces premature studies.
Decision-oriented	Decisions	Provide a knowledge & value base for making & defending decisions.	Encourages use of evaluation to plan & implement needed	Necessary collaboration between evaluator & decision-maker provides

			programmes. Helps justify decisions about plans & actions.	opportunity to bias results.
Policy studies	Broad issues	Identify and assess potential costs & benefits of competing policies.	Provide general direction for broadly focused actions.	Often corrupted or subverted by politically motivated actions of participants.
Consumer-oriented	Generalized needs & values, effects	Judge the relative merits of alternative goods & services.	Independent appraisal to protect practitioners & consumers from shoddy products & services. High public credibility.	Might not help practitioners do a better job. Requires credible & competent evaluators.
Accreditation/ certification	Standards & guidelines	Determine if institutions, programmes, & personnel should be approved to perform specified functions.	Helps public make informed decisions about quality of organizations & qualifications of personnel.	Standards & guidelines typically emphasize intrinsic criteria to the exclusion of outcome measures.
Connoisseur	Critical guideposts	Critically describe, appraise, & illuminate an object.	Exploits highly developed expertise on subject of interest. Can inspire others to more insightful efforts.	Dependent on small number of experts, making evaluation susceptible to subjectivity, bias, and corruption.

Adversary Evaluation	"Hot" issues	Present the pros & cons of an issue.	Ensures balances presentations of represented perspectives.	Can discourage cooperation, heighten animosities.
Client-centred	Specific concerns & issues	Foster understanding of activities & how they are valued in a given setting & from a variety of perspectives.	Practitioners are helped to conduct their own evaluation.	Low external credibility, susceptible to bias in favour of participants.

Note: Adapted and condensed primarily from House (1978) and Stufflebeam & Webster (1980).

1.7 Techniques and Tools of Evaluation

In order to gather information we require tools and techniques. These should be valid, reliable and usable. The interpretation of gathered information needs to be specified in numerical scores, grades as well as in qualitative terms. Judgment should be made both on scholastic aspects as well as on co-scholastic aspects which depend to a large extent on the learning atmosphere and learning mores of an institution.

As far as interpretation is concerned, attainment can be measured in terms of three levels. First is with reference to the learner himself/herself and the existing rank of progress. The learning gaps need to be recognized and marked upon. The second level is to classify the status of the learner with reference to his/her peer group. (Percentile Rank) The third level is with reference to the criteria. The criteria mean the expected level of learning keeping in view the required skills.

An evaluation tool is a means of appraisal scientifically designed to evaluate or measure what is required to be evaluated or measured. Following factors need to be considered while using a tool:

Balance	Objectivity	Discrimination	Relevance
Fairness	Validity	Speed	Reliability

Some specific tools of evaluation are:

Anecdotal Record:	*Rating Scale:*	*Aptitude:*	*Inventories:*	*Teacher Made and Standardized Tests:*
It is used to approach the past behaviour of the students.	It is used to allocate opinions and judgment regarding situations, objects etc.	They are used to measure potential performance and special ability of students.	These are used to assess the expression of inward feelings of individuals through questionnaires etc.	They are used to measure in numerical terms the attainment of the students in various school subjects.

Techniques of Evaluation consist of test and other items for measuring growth in particular outcomes of learning. Tools are the instruments used for measuring the learning outcome such as question papers, observation schedules, rating scale, checklists etc. For example, while observation is a technique a checklist is a tool. Information can be best collected about children in 'natural' settings. Some information is based on teachers' observations about learners in the course of teaching. Other information is based on planned and purposeful observation of students on activities/tasks.

1. Observation

Subject matter can be best gathered about children in '*natural*' settings. Some information is based on teachers' observations about learners in the course of teaching. Other information is based on planned and purposeful observation of students on activities/tasks.

Merits of Observation

- Through observations various aspects of personality development can be accessed.

- Observations can be used to evaluate individuals as well as groups.
- Through observations assessments can be made during varying time periods.
- Evidence of child's performance/knowledge is based on an '*on-the-spot record*'.
- Over time, elaborated observations of behaviour as well as interests, challenges, patterns/trends appear which permit teachers to create a comprehensive picture/view of the child.

Threats Regarding Observation

- Avoid arriving at inferences/interpretations or jumping to conclusions. It is important to take down more than what is actually seen.
- Dependent on the ability of the observer which determine '*what*' is observed.
- Requires sensitivity and simplicity in the way the observation is done.
- Observations to be made over a period of time, across different activities and settings.

2. Projects

These are undertaken over a period of time and generally incorporate collection and analysis of data. Projects are useful in theme-based tasks to be accomplished as class work and/or homework in groups. They can be open ended or structured and can be both individual and group projects. They should be based on matter outside the textbooks and related to the child's environment/culture/lifestyle/community based social programmes.

Merits of Projects

- Projects provide opportunities to look into and work with one's hands.
- Observe, collect data, examine, organize and interpret data and draw generalizations.

- Provides an opportunity to work in groups and in real life situations.
- Helps evolve a positive attitude towards group work, sharing and learning from each other.

Threats Regarding Projects

- The nature and difficulty level of the projects should be such that students can brawl it by themselves.
- Materials to be utilized for the project should be available in the school, neighbourhood or home setting.
- These should not put a financial burden on the parents.
- Each school could go in for a Resource Centre, which would have locally accessible materials.

3. Questions

An exemplary way of finding out what children know, think, imagine, and feel. The learners can be accessed through questions and problems. Even the ability to make a set of questions for given answers is a valid test of learning. A teacher can in the course of teaching as part of formative Assessment come to know of learning difficulties in children by asking questions that make children think.

Characteristics of a good question

- A question should be based on a predetermined objective and should be framed in such a way that it tests the objective effectively.
- It should stipulate a specific task through the instructions. For this, appropriate directional words should be used, and structured situation should be given.
- It should show the limit and the scope of the answer (length of the answer) in conformity with the estimated time and marks allotted to it.
- The question should test the aforesaid area of content which it intends to test.
- A good question is framed in a clear, precise and unambiguous language, well within the understanding of the students.

- A question should be written keeping in view the level the students for whom it is meant. The difficulty of the question depends upon the ability to be tested, the content area to be tested and the time available to answer it.
- A good question must distinguish between bright students and others.
- The language of the question should be specific and precise so that the scope of the expected answer is clearly delimited or defined.
- Value points or marks carried by a question as a whole and also its sub parts should be clearly mentioned.

Types of Questions

(a) Supply Type Questions

In this type of questions student has to supply the answer. The answer may vary from one word to several paragraphs. Such type of questions is also called as '*free-response*' questions. Supply-type questions may be divided into four categories–*essay type, short answer type, very short answer type and fill in the blanks type questions.*

(b) Essay Type Questions

The term essay expresses a written response which may exist of one or two pages. The student is allowed to have freedom with respect to wording, length and organization of the answer. A distinction should be made between the essay type question used to measure knowledge and the essay type question employed to test writing skills in languages, which is called a composition test.

(c) Constructing Essay Type Questions

Essay type questions usually begin with such terms as '*discuss*', '*explain*', '*evaluate*', '*define*', '*compare*', '*contrast*', '*describe*', etc. Essay type questions are cracking when the group to be tested is small and restricted time is available for test preparation. It is also quite suitable to test written expression.

Some sample essay type questions are as under:

1. Why do Muslims believe that the Prophet Muhammad is the final prophet? Explain?
2. Discuss the different kinds of prayer that Muslims practice?
3. If Islam is considered to be a religion of peace, then why there are so much conflict in countries where Muslims live?
4. What factors contributed to the rise of Islamic fundamentalism? Give your comments?

(d) Short Answer Type Questions

Essay type questions suffer from deficiency of objectivity and reliability while objective type questions cannot be used for testing certain aspects of growth like the ability to express in brief, summarize and organize the ideas in precise manner. Short answer questions are a good via-media between the two extremes. If understood and framed properly, they have the advantages of both the objective type and essay type questions.

1. What is Jihad?
2. What is the difference between the words "Islam", and "Islamic"?
3. What are the foundational sources of Islamic beliefs and practices?
4. Is the Qur'an read only in Arabic?

(e) Very Short Answer Type Questions

- Very short answer questions are those which have one specific testing point and can be marked quite objectively.
- More content can be tested through these questions and more reliability and validity can be ensured.
- It helps in testing knowledge of the examinee by asking him to supply a word, phrase, or a figure or a sentence which is required for answering the questions.
- It can be answered in one word to one sentence.
- It mostly takes one to two minutes to answer and the range of marks allotted is half to one mark.

- Very short answer questions can be used profitably in all the school subjects.
- There are many types of very short answer questions, some are given below:

(i) **Completion Type: It is useful for testing expression in language testing.**
Q. Qur'an is the holy ....

(ii) **Analogy type:**
Q. Muslim: Qur'an Hindu: ....

(iii) **Location Type: In Geography such questions can be used for testing map skills.**
Q. Show on the map– Makkah, Hira' Cave.

(iv) **Fill in the Blanks Type:**
In this type of question a statement is provided. In which one word or two words at different places are removed and students are asked to fill in the blanks with appropriate words. An example of this type is given below:
Masjid al-Haram is the .... mosque in the world surrounded by the holiest places of Islam. (Largest)

(f) Selection Type Questions

In these types of questions students are expected to answer them by selecting the correct answer among the provided choices. Such questions are also known as objective type questions. These may be divided into alternative response type, matching type and multiple choice type questions, etc.

Selection type questions are all objective type questions. Objective type questions have only one correct answer which the student has to choose out of the given choices. As these questions can be marked objectively, they are called objective type questions. This means that the examinee will get the same marks no matter who evaluates the question. They can be scored mechanically and that is why these are very popular particularly in a situation when large number of candidates is to be tested. The following are different forms of objective type questions.

(g) Alternate Response Type

In these types of questions students have to select one out of two alternatives as a correct answer. The different type of alternative response questions are as under:

(a) True/False or Yes/No

In this type of question a statement is given and the candidate is asked whether it is true or false (T/F). True/False questions are easy to construct and score. They provide a fairly reliable measure of students understanding particularly in the classroom testing.

(b) Write 'T' if the statement is 'True' and 'F' if the statement is 'False'

The people who follow the religion of Islam are known as Islamic. T... F ....

The religion of Islam condones the oppression of women. T... F ....

(c) Right /Wrong type or Yes/no Type

Put tick (✓) mark if statement is Right and (×) if Wrong.

> Muslims are allowed to go anytime to fulfil their hajj or pilgrimage.

(d) Matching Type

In matching type questions there are two columns. The words or statements given in column one are to be matched with the answers given in column two. The matching type question may be of the following type:

(i) Single Matching

In this type of question two columns are used. In left column stimuli are presented whereas in right column responses are given. Students are asked to match the response with a given stimulus.

(ii) Direction

Match the words given in Column A with Column B to make a correct pair. *(Sample)*

	Column A	*Column B*
A	Al-Aqsa Mosque	Jerusalem
B	Kaaba	Mecca
C	Namaz	Muslim

(e) Multiple Choices

Multiple choice items are the most useful of all the objective type items. In these questions there is a stem which poses the problem. The stem may be in question form or in the form of an incomplete statement. Then there are four or five choices given for an answer. The student has to select the correct answer from the given alternatives.

1. The term "Islam" means
   a. Submission
   b. Peace
   c. Fortitude
   d. Thankfulness
2. Which of the following is *not* an essential part of Islamic belief?
   a. The belief in the oneness of God
   b. The belief in the Day of Judgment
   c. The belief in sorcery
   d. The belief in prophets

4. Checklists

A checklist a type of job aid used to reduce failure by compensating for potential limits of human memory and attention. It helps to ensure consistency and completeness in carrying out a task. A basic example is the "to do list." A more advanced checklist would be a schedule, which lays out tasks to be done according to time of day or other factors. A primary task in checklist is documentation of the task and auditing against the documentation.

Merits of Checklists

- Quick and easy to implement.
- Provides particular information about specific objectives.
- Can point towards a course of how and when skills have been acquired by the child as well as a group of children.

Concerns regarding Checklists

- Limited information, only indicating presence of a skill.
- Does not show child's response to different situations or provide specific examples of responses.
- Does not provide information about context.
- Can at times become awkward because of the number of specific items.

5. Portfolio

Collection of evidences of students' work over a period of time. It could be day-to-day work or selection of the learner's best piece of work.

Advantages of Portfolio

- Provide a cumulative record. In the process, a picture of how a skill or knowledge area develops appears.
- Enables the student to demonstrate to others, his/her learning and progress.
- The child becomes a progressive participant in learning and appraisal.

Concerns regarding Checklists Portfolio

- Prime work to be put into the Portfolio should have a specific reason.
- Not all papers/items of work are to be included. This will become unmanageable.

6. Narrative Records

Teacher/child peers write a narrative statement of the learner's experiences. These give the opportunity for investigating every aspect of the child's life and can be used with anecdotal evidences for creating a more holistic image of the learner and can be used to develop Cumulative Records.

7. Photographs

Provides documentation of a learner's experiences, while they are doing tasks/work. They could also be of finished products, projects models etc.

Advantages of Photographs

- Provide accurate recall of circumstance.
- Provides an insight into children's ways of reasoning and interacting.
- Alleviate sharing of information with families.
- Provides an insight into the child's emotional, social and psychological prospect of development.

Concerns regarding Photographs

- The aesthetic quality may not be critical.
- Avoid making the child self-conscious in front of the camera by your comments or suggestions.

8. Paintings and other Examples of Artistic Endeavour

Provides evidence of a learner's abilities, thoughts and attitudes. Finished products, project models etc. can be incorporated into the child's Portfolio to provide evidence of the learner's ability.

9. Videos

Provides documentation of a learner's experiences, while they are task/engaged with a project. They could also be of finished products, projects models etc.

Advantages of Videos

- Both permit language and the way it is used to be '*captured*' with accuracy.
- Movement and sound add to the understanding of the events taking place.
- Helps to understand student's explanations that indicate various ways of thinking.

Concerns Regarding Videos

- Analysis is time consuming,
- Children may occasionally be '*performing*' for the camera.
- Costly as it requires technical expertise.

10. Rating Scales

By a rating is meant the judgment of one person by another. Rating is a term applied to expression of opinion or judgment regarding some situation, object or character. Opinions are usually expressed on a scale or values. Rating techniques are devices by which such judgments may be quantified. A rating scale is a method by which we systematize the expression of opinion concerning a trait. The ratings are done by parents, teachers, a board of interviewers and judges and by the self as well.

There are two characteristics of a rating scale. Description of the characteristics to be rated, and some methods by which the quality, frequency or importance of each item to be rated may be given. Provide a comparative record of the learner's level of achievement can prove to be counterproductive. They should be used judiciously and discreetly.

11. Anecdotal Records

An Anecdotal Record is the observed behaviour of a child. It is defined as a record of some significant item of conduct, a record of an episode in the life of the student; a word picture of the student in action, a word snapshot at the moment of the incident; any narration of events in which the student takes such a part as to reveal something which may be significant about his personality.

Anecdotal record is a running cumulative description of actual examples of behaviour as observed by teachers and counsellor. The description of the behaviour is followed by a comment by the teacher. An example will make it clear:

Place: English class.

Objective Description: I have been finding Ravi/Rashida day after day in the library reading magazines, yet she/he never has time to correct revise/edit or to work carefully on English assignments.

Comment: Ravi/Rashida does not like to write but likes to read. I have asked the librarian not to admit him/her during his/her free periods unless he hears from me that Ravi/Rashida has done all work regarding assignments.

Uses and Values of Anecdotal Records

- They provide specific description of personality and minimize generalizations.
- They are very helpful in understanding the child's behaviour in diverse situations.
- They provide a continuous record.
- They provide data for learners to use in self-appraisal.
- A summary of these records is valuable for forwarding with a pupil when he is transferred from one school to another.
- The new members of the staff may use these records and acquaint themselves with the student body.
- These records aid in clinical service.
- They stimulate teachers to use the records.

12. Essays etc.

Provides evidence of a learner's abilities related to expression mirroring one's abilities, thoughts and attitudes. Finished products, project models etc. can be incorporated into the learner's Portfolio to provide evidence of the learner's ability.

13. Student Interviews and Oral Tests

- Allows the learner to participate in the learning assessment process.

- These can test abilities like pronunciation, intonation, and accent.
- Students cannot dodge the examiners as they can be cross-questioned.
- Oral tests should not test the items which can be tested through written examination.
- Oral tests being individual are time consuming.

Conversations

Helps us learn what/how the learner thinks, knows and imagines. Helps to lest listening and speaking skills.

14. Examination, Tests, Quizzes, Competitions

Tells us how well a learner remembers what he has been taught and what he has learnt.

15. Narrative Reports

The idea should not be to reduce the learner to a set of letters. They can give a more comprehensive report of the learner in a holistic manner. Reports can be incorporated into Portfolios.

However no single assessment tool/method is capable of providing information/evidence about learner's progress and learning in different areas of development. While teaching, a teacher realizes that a lot can be understood from observing learners, listening to them, discussing informally with their peers and parents as well as talking to other teachers, reviewing written work (class work and homework) done by learner and using self-assessments by them. Teachers use different methods. All that is required is that a judicious and predictable combination of various tools be adopted to give as accurate information about the child as possible.

1.8 Discussions and Conclusion

In reflection to what presented about place of evaluation in Islam and its importance and necessity, we can understand that evaluation has a special importance in education specially in teaching. This necessity will be cleared more while it would be looked from Islam point of view so that educational system can be reached to goal of Islamic education which is human perfection. Considering to what discussed about specifications of Islamic evaluation like self-evaluation, plurality of evaluation tools, speed in evaluation, consideration to individual differences and deviation from mistake and changing sentence, it is proposing to:

- Due to make responsibility and self-confidence in students during education, there should be conditions for involving learners in evaluation process.
- Use different tools based on educational goals and characteristics of learners.
- Encouraging the social position and increasing the knowledge level and skills of teachers as the most important persons in evaluation position, should be placed in priority of education plans and activities.
- The individual differences should be considered by planners and teachers.
- An Educational specialist and researcher should find out the scientific criterions in field of evaluation by using Islamic religious teaching and perform of realization of these criterions by informing and teaching the executers of educational system.
- The culture of consideration to these principles in educational system should be developed by holding seminars, making articles and encouraging to writing about position of evaluation in Islam and its principles.

REFERENCES

Charles, S. and Brain, D. (2017). *Handbook on Measurement, Assessment and Evaluation in Higher Education.* Rutledge.

Ebrahimi A., Khanjarkhani Z. and Morovati Z. (2011). *Study of Islamic perspectives about evaluation criterions and its educative points*. J. Life Sci. Biomed. 1(1): 18-23.

Kenneth, D. (1998). *Educational and Psychological Measurement and Evaluation.* Allyn & Bacon, University of Michigan.

Paresh, B.A. (2015). *Educational Measurement and Evaluation.* Canadian Academic Publishing.

Rani, J.S. (2004). *Educational Measurement and Evaluation*, Discovery Publishing House.

Marzuki, P., (2009). *Yogakarta*, Debut Wahana Press & FISE UNY.

Taimiyah, I. (1961). *Kitab al-iman,* Damaskus, Dar al-Fikr.

file:///C:/Users/DRC36/Downloads/929-Article%20Text-1868-1-10-20170223.pdf retrieved on 01/05/18 2:20pm

https://www.atsdr.cdc.gov/communityengagement/pdf/pce_report_chapter_7_ shef.pdf retrieved on 05/05/18 12:20am

https://blog.socialcops.com/academy/7-types-of-evaluation/ retrieved on 07/05/18 11:26pm

12
Lesson Planning in Teaching of Islam

Brenny Novriansyah and *Nasrin*

"*The most loved teacher by their students was a teacher who well-planned before delivering lesson*"

As like constructing an apartment, engineers almost conducting preparation through model and building design in details. Those conducted to ensure all parts of building could accommodate the necessity of building owner along with its beauty, arts, safety, comfortable, and socio-cultural aspects of people who are living in.

Teacher as a facilitator of student's learning should do the same in preparing lesson planning as a guideline of teaching process within classroom whether the process conducted inside or outside the classroom. Teacher assigned to conduct teaching process in proper manner and viable to maximize fruitful gains of time periods of teaching. Just like drama performance, the synopsis in the first minutes of shows as an introduction of story and then, second phase shows the beginning story, third phase shows the main character of story, and the fourth as the last phase tells the moral messages of performance.

Furthermore, teaching process has been sometimes allocated 40 minutes per-period. Teacher had to establish learning effectively within 40 minutes and manage to seduce and captivate students in classroom to learn persistently. Hence, managing classroom properly would create pleasant and satisfaction of students towards learning process.

Lesson planning helps teacher to know in advance the subject material and the mode of its teaching through classroom. The ideas in planning would inspire teacher of how to begin the learning, how to arrange the pupils, how to rob their anticipation fully concentrate to learning, how to correlate the concept of material to real life, how to summarize the lesson along with its evaluation.

Now, hope you get the main point of this discussion, that designing lesson plan was extremely important before conducting teaching practice. So, the writing will discuss about meaning and concept of lesson planning in teaching of Islam, types, significance, proper approach of lesson planning for teaching of Islam and some models.

Meaning and Concept of Lesson Planning in Teaching of Islam

There will be various meaning and concept of lesson planning, but here we will find proper meaning in terms of teaching of Islam, as you are looking for. In Collin English Dictionary, lesson plan means a plan, used by teacher in school, detailing structure and format of lesson. Lesson plan was a detail of instruction for classroom of one subject material. Whether the subject material is same, one lesson plan could be used in many classrooms but in different schools.

Kochar (1984) argued that lesson planning was actually a plan of teaching action, which includes the working philosophy of teacher, his knowledge of philosophy, information and understanding about pupils, comprehension of the objectives of education, knowledge of materials to be taught, ability and skills in selecting effective method and conducting an art of teaching.

Aggarwal (2001) argued that lesson planning is essentially an experience in anticipatory teaching, which involves teacher's experience, mental and emotional in advance. The teacher will experience in imagination and thereafter fully tinge with realism upon the eager faces, the questions that will arise, the difficulties the pupils will encounter and the way these difficulties are to be met.

According to Banga (2012), planning is very essential not only in teaching but in all spheres of life. Planning of a lesson in advance is the fundamental condition for the success of lesson process. A lesson plan is a teaching outline consists of important points of subject materials to be presented in classroom. The lesson plan may include objectives, points to be asked, references to materials and assignment, etc., it may carry subject matter in advance along with mode of its delivery in the classroom.

Lesson plan was a guide of teaching-learning process made by teacher to gain the aims of learning in proper way. Sharma (2013) stated that lesson plan is simply a story of the way of how teacher deliver the materials towards students and to keep his students busy during a particular period. It indicates what and how the teacher and his pupils are going to do in that period.

On the other hand, Wikipedia (2018) defined a lesson plan as a description of teacher's details of course and instruction or learning trajectory for learning. The development of lesson plan will vary and depends on the preference of the teacher, subject being covered, and the need of the students. Some requirements and mandated order by school system and government rule in education could also be added. Hence, the lesson plan was useful as teacher's guide in running particular lesson that covered what the students are supposed to learn, how the goal will be reached and a way of measuring the achievement of learning through homework, test, worksheet, etc.

The mandate and requirements of school system or government rules related to education might be added in lesson plan such as environmental issues and solution to be undertaken by people was added in lesson plan to achieve the goal of state in human resources that aware to environmental problems.

Problems in Teaching of Islam

Teacher of Islamic studies subject should aware to the difference of Muslim cultures and understanding towards the teaching of Islam. The difference of Mazhab and Imam as their priest, might also create the difference in accepting the materials. Sometimes, teachers got complaint from parents and Muslim community surround the school regarding teaching of Islam those are opposite to their understanding and not suitable to their culture.

Maunah (2009) stated that the obstacles in learning Islamic studies and Islamic morals depend on its specific character. Islamic teaching was taught not only as knowledge base but also as belief. Teaching Islam as belief had become problem in part of teaching methods and tolerance to student's schools' discrepancy. We sometimes rarely found parents protest against the teacher who did wrong in teaching mathematics to their children but in opposite of that we often found parents protest the teacher who taught their children different schools as their parent's belief and assumed mistaken in teaching religion.

Religious belief is being sensitive in teaching, so teachers have to aware in making lesson plan. Whenever the students implement the *ibadaat* practices which are opposite to their parent's understanding. The parent with all of his power and knowledge will blame the school and teachers who teach wrong teachings to their children. Students then, might be confused between which are correct and incorrect.

The complaint seldom comes in *fiqh furu'iyat* or debatable Islamic law, which raise the dissent opinions of scholars or *ikhtilaaf ulama'*. In this case, teacher should have bright knowledge regarding *furu'iyat* and be susceptible upon where the students are commonly living and what are generally their tradition and *mazhab*.

Arranging lesson planning in teaching of Islam should be careful towards sensitive topics in Islam, which will raise complaint and debatable arguments from parents. Unlike teaching sciences, whenever the teacher delivered something wrong in formula and answer of worksheets, the parent would not do complaint to school but only provide the correct answer to worksheets.

The concept of Lesson Planning in teaching of Islam is shown in Fig. 12.1.

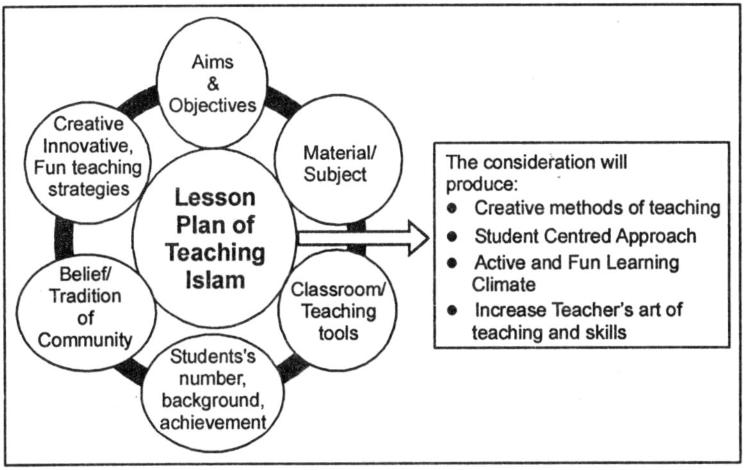

Fig. 12.1: Aspects should be aware by teachers in designing Lesson Plan in Teaching of Islam.

Various Subjects in Teaching of Islam

Each Madarsa and school has different kind of curriculum in teaching of Islam. Some public schools only teach Islamic studies as a subsidiary subject and some others completely teach Islam in separate subjects. Whereas Madarsa with his curriculum was designed 70 per cent of subjects are related to Islamic studies. Those various Islamic subjects almost taught in traditional method of teaching practice. Moreover, the teacher who assigned in teaching were senior teacher and still cling firmly to learning methods that he assumed as a successful method in learning the subject as based on his own experience when he was a student in Madarsa.

Teaching of Islam in Madarsa of Indonesia practically sourced from Ministry of Religious Affairs Curriculum that covers Aqeeda Akhlaq, Fiqh, Qur'an and Hadith, Islamic History of Culture, and Arabic. In opposite of Public Madarsa, schools under management of Ministry of Education and Culture had also implemented Islamic studies for Muslim students. The Islamic studies subject in public schools covered general Islamic teaching practice as the basic knowledge for students. Furthermore, Islamic Boarding Schools, which have their own curriculum and provide completely sciences, arts, and Islamic teachings subjects. The teaching of Islam in Islamic Boarding School was taught separately in details i.e. Fiqh, Tawheed, History of Islam, Ushul Fiqh, Hadith, Qur'an, Qur'anic Interpretation, Nahwu, Saraf, Balagha, Musthalah ul Hadith, and etc.

Those curriculum was designated by Ministry of Religious Affairs of The Republic of Indonesia along with lesson plan form, teacher's handbooks, student's books, and teaching tools which circulated to all public schools, Madarsas and Islamic Boarding Schools.

Hence, school or Madarsa inspectors have to acknowledge Madarsa teachers in designing good and proper lesson plan for teaching various Islamic studies subjects. Senior teacher should not design lesson plan in a way of memorizing, it will cause the learning process not creative and will gain the same level achievement than before. The creativity of teaching methods and instructional strategies would increase student's fondness towards Islamic studies and do not feel being forced.

Significance of Lesson Planning in Teaching of Islam

Naqvi (2010) stated that teacher's approach towards the students should be shaped by their own state of mind and mindset towards the very process of teaching-learning. Whenever in their mind the students just feel being repulsive and irritating. Those teachers neither think of motivating students to learn nor preparing lesson plan in the required manner. It shows from the way the teacher begins teaching process. Where students were asked to open the book and merely commanded to follow the instruction as like robots.

The fact matter showed that lesson plan is an essential part of teaching process. The proper plan will influence students' learning motivation and the fruitful of learning process. Lesson plan would transform allocated time of teaching periods, materials into learning activities, proper teaching method to gain learning objectives and instructional strategies developed in classroom.

Well-planned teaching process will create pleasant appearance in classrooms. Students are motivated to learn and arrange learning tools neatly beside them like books, notebook, sharpening pencils, eraser, and etc. before teacher enters the classroom. The well-planned teachers had increased their confidence and mastery of materials. So, the students felt their progress after learning the subject. Whenever the students felt any progressive matters after learning the subject, they would be satisfied with their effort in learning. So, the higher learning satisfaction they got, the higher they are motivated to learn new things.

The lesson plan affects the teacher's skill, intelligence, ability and his personality while teaching process. The following are the chief functions of lesson planning in teaching of Islam:

1. It delimits the field of work of the teacher as well as of the students and provides a definite objective for each day's work either in schools, Madarsa or Boarding Schools.
2. As the objectives of learning were determined, the teacher gets impetus to realize learning achievement.
3. The lesson plan either tends to prevent wandering from the subject and going off the way or could make teaching systematic, orderly and more efficient rather than only reading materials and let the students hear what the teacher

reads. It serves as a check on the possible wastage of time and energy of the teachers and students.

4. Lesson Planning helps the teacher in organizing and systematizing the upcoming learning process. Learning activities are interconnected and associated and the continuity of deductive process is ensured.
5. Lesson Planning could avoid needless repetition and missing materials of Islamic teachings.
6. Planning helps the teacher to overcome the feeling of nervousness and insecurity during the learning process and gives him confidence to face the class.
7. Lesson planning gives chances to the teacher to memorize the Qur'an and Hadith prepositions and to think out new ways and means of making the lesson interesting and to introduce thought-provoking questions.
8. Lesson planning ensures a definite assignment for class and availability of adequate materials for the lesson.
9. Lesson planning enables the teacher to link the new knowledge with the previous knowledge acquired by students, especially regarding Qur'an and Hadith prepositions to be memorized by students.
10. Lesson planning strengthens a proper connection between new materials with the previous materials, because learning Islam should be connected between each topic.
11. Lesson planning enables the teacher to prepare a suitable scheme of selection and organization of subject-matter, materials and activities.
12. Lesson planning enables the teacher to prepare pivotal questions and illustrations regarding *akhlak*, *Ibadaat,* etc.
13. Lesson planning helps the teachers as well as the taught in fixing new learning by making adequate provision for drill work, practice and revision.

Thus, teaching of Islam should change the approach methods and instructional strategies to be more fun, creative, and concern to student centred approach.

Principles of Lesson Planning in Teaching of Islam

Lesson planning is important thing to do by the teacher before conducting teaching practice in classroom to reduce the mistakes and something remains as a fatal of unpreparedness. The lesson planning envisages as a blueprint and a guide map of teaching actions. It is based on operational philosophy of teacher, teacher's understanding of his pupils, teacher's knowledge of the material to be taught and teacher's knowledge of the methods of teaching.

Some of the principles in the beneath might be helpful in preparing lesson planning for teachers of Islamic studies:

1. Teacher should aware student's need and not material's need. So, one lesson planning sometimes could be used in many classrooms but in multiple academic years that are vary in needs and demand. Teacher of Islamic studies should be flexible in teaching, as the lesson planning was a guide of teaching but teacher must be careful to do not return back to previous traditional approach and left the lesson plan behind.
2. Teacher of Islamic studies must have mastery of Qur'an and Hadith recitation or *fashaahat ul-qiraat*, and memorize some verses and Hadith related to topics, as it is urgently required in teaching of Islam in any subject.
3. Teacher must keep abreast with the new methods and latest instructional strategies and provide attractive teaching tools in teaching of Islam.
4. Knowing student's needs and understanding student's traits and interests were better rather than merely teaching them in a logical fashion.
5. Student can learn from various competences like reading, listening, watching, writing and doing. Since monotony is a drawback, so teacher should provide various learning activities in one topic of learning particularly with young pupils.

Approaches in Lesson Planning

There will be various steps in designing lesson plan. It depends on which approaches being selected and considered suitable to student's needs. The suitable approaches to lesson planning in teaching of Islam are:

1. The Herbertian approach or five steps approach (Herbert).
2. The Project approach (C. Dewey and Kilpatrick).
3. The Morison approach/unit approach or cyclic plan of teaching (Henry C. Morison).
4. The Gloverian approach.
5. The Evaluation approach (Dr. B.S. Bloom).
6. The Indian Approach i.e. RCEM approach (Regional College of Education Mysore approach) and NCERT.

Here we will not discuss about each approach but the detailed discussion on lesson planning approaches will be provided in different book. Let's go to steps of lesson planning.

Steps of Lesson Planning

Mere than story, lesson planning indicates previous knowledge upon which it is based belong to students. It should look more like a programme that contains headings and sub-headings, providing different things to be conducted at different stages, the instruments and material to be provided, all activities to be undertaken and the knowledge and information to be imparted and learnt by students.

The steps of lesson planning arranged as based on different approaches depends on what the objectives and materials to be taught and student's needs. For teaching of Islam effectively, the teacher has to proceed the learning in systematic manner. Let's now discuss those steps, which may help you in preparing a lesson plan in teaching of Islam.

Here are steps of lesson planning according to Herbertian approach, Project approach and Morison approach:

Table: Different Steps of Lesson Planning approaches (Banga, 2012)

Herbertian Approach	*Project Approach*	*Morison Approach*
Preparation	Creating the Situation	Exploration
Presentation or Method	Proposing and Choosing the Project	Presentation
Association or Comparison	Planning the Project	Assimilation
Generalisation	Execution of the Project	Organization
Application	Evaluation of the Project	Recitation
Recapitulation	Recording of the Project	

At least, the following 5 steps of lesson planning in teaching of Islam are acceptable to teachers:

1. Formulation of educational objectives; the first step to do by teacher is to know the objectives of learning should be achieved by students. Teacher has to find the aims of lesson along with objectives. Finding the formulation of objectives should be begun from questions asked by himself. Those questions like:

   a. What do I want my students know when they leave the classroom?
   b. What are the targets should be achieved for today?
   c. Are these aims suitable to students?
   d. Are these objectives related to the previous lesson?

Teacher should know that the formulation of learning objectives would be determined in their relationship to learning aims.

2. Selection and organization of content; Now in the second step, teacher should ask himself about:
   a. What kind of content will be selected to achieve the intended objectives and aims?
   b. What are Qur'an and Hadith arguments/*dalil* relevant to content? Teacher should remember that teaching of Islam is not merely delivering the knowledge but also to increase their faith/*imaan* to Islam and to conduct the obedience and command of Allah.
   c. What strategies would be established to make the lesson meaningful and correlate them with the real life? As per Islam was the way of life, hence teacher should correlate all contents to real life of students, their family and social facts.
   d. How much time will be spent in apperception, reading, discussion, review, practical work and test? Instead of delivering materials in monotonous way and presenting waste things not related to objectives.
   e. How will you start the lesson? First impression imparts enjoyment and fun in learning. Warm smile, friendly, and motivation will be useful throughout the lesson. Proper method of teaching and instructional strategies selected will create effective classroom climate.

f. What kind of teaching aids will be best to use? As teaching of Islam sometimes related to norms, behaviour, and ethics, hence selecting some stories related to topics will be more effective to make them understand how to implement the norms in their life. Not all of content materials need aids, unless using pictures in purpose of making learning more attractive is acceptable.

g. Which kind of evaluation will be used such as quiz, test, homework, portfolio, and Verse or Hadith recitation.

3. Motivation of preparation; the third step is preparing the way how teacher enhances student's will and interest to learn. Generally, the instructional strategies which concern on student centred and using teaching aids such as: *janazat* doll, compass, water, poster, pictures, PPT, etc. including student's involvement through drama, practical assignment, and discussion mostly motivate students to learn materials. Using LCD projector sometimes is more effective to capture student's interest to learn materials, especially in teaching Qur'an and Hadith recitation and tajweed. Moreover teacher with skillful in writing Arabic (Qur'an and Hadith) on board will also capture student's anticipation towards materials. Students will try hardly to draw the writings as well as teacher's writing.

The pupils should be active participants in the classrooms. Teacher required to anticipate; how many questions are raised from students?, who are of students taking too much part in discussion and who are not?, which students are being neglegted?

4. Recapitulation and assignment; the fourth step is arranging the way of how to elaborate the summary of lesson. Teacher must provide the strategy that helps students to view the conclusion of materials related to lesson. Pupils are required to express their opinion of materials summary and reproduce the materials learnt.

Assignment will be very useful to know how their understanding was regarding materials. Teachers have to provide worksheets, paper test, and homework and group assignment to ensure student achievement related to materials.

Evaluating a lesson; after completing lesson, teacher has to ask some questions to himself regarding teaching of Islam established. Those questions will be useful either for teacher in arranging the next lesson plan or for school inspector in finding information regarding teachers' ability in teaching. The questions as like in the following table:

No.	*Questions*	*Yes*	*No*	*Comment*
a.	The motivation is effective for all pupils			
b.	I can maintain the motivation throughout the lesson			
c.	Aims are clear to the students			
d.	My questions are well distributed			
e.	There are questions from students			
f.	I use effective audio-visual aids			
g.	I am able to satisfy and challenge the superior students			
h.	There is enough pupils participation			
i.	I include homework or assignment			

Lesson Planning in Teaching of Islam: An Example

Before arranging lesson planning, teacher should have some questions around their head to be considered, those questions will be the mainstream of thought in designing the teaching process that hopes to occur. Now, let's see what are the questions which should come to teachers during planning:

1. What are the needs, difficulties, problems and interests of the students? Knowing the students will be easier for teacher to teach in the classrooms.
2. What way the requirements of the subject matter suitable to the capacity and growth of the students?
3. What preparation have the students made for attacking the subject?
4. What is their previous knowledge, which can be correlated to the present learning?
5. How can the subject matter be presented more effective and efficient?
6. What type of teaching aids should be prepared?
7. What type of application work should be used to make real the grasp of the students of the objectives of the lesson?
8. What methods should be used to make the students' participants in the lesson?

The preliminary information related to lesson and pupils almost required in lesson plan arrangement. Here are the examples of lesson plan in teaching of Islam:

LESSON 1

This lesson planning is often used in public schools.

Subject	:	Islamic Studies
Topic	:	The Decline of Qur'an
Date and time	:	01.02.2018, 12.00 p.m.
Name of Teacher	:	Muhammad
Name of the school	:	S.T.S School
Topic of the lesson	:	The Decline of Qur'an

1. Aims:
2. Objectives:
3. Background Knowledge:
4. Teaching aids:
5. Introduction:
6. Statement of the aim:
7. Development:
8. Recapitulation:
9. Summary:

LESSON 2

This lesson planning is sometimes used in Madarsa.

Subject	:	Fiqh
Topic	:	*Thahara*/purification
Date and time	:	01.10.2018, 12.00 p.m.
Name of Teacher	:	Bilal
Name of the school	:	S.T.S School
Topic of the lesson	:	*Thahara*/purification

1. Aims:
2. Objectives:
3. Background Knowledge:
4. Teaching aids:
5. Introduction:
6. Statement of the aim:
7. Development:
8. Recapitulation:
9. Summary:

LESSON 3

The lesson planning below was designed plan belong to Indonesia schools and Madarsas. You can find similarities and differences:

Subject	:	Environmental Education
Topic	:	Water Pollution
School Name	:	Public/Private Secondary Madrasa
Class/Semester	:	X / 2nd
Unit	:	1. Water Pollution
Sub-unit	:	1.3. Ways to Save Water Sources as Per Islamic Principles
Session	:	2
Allocated time	:	45 minutes

A. Core Competences

1. Appreciate and practice the teaching of their religion **(Spiritual Quotient/Metaphysic).**
2. Appreciate and practice the honest behaviour, discipline, responsibility, caring (cooperation, tolerance, peace) polite, responsive, and pro-active, and displayed as part of the solution to various problems in interacting effectively with social and natural environment as well as in placing himself as a reflection of the nation in the world association **(Emotional Quotient/Attitude).**

3. Understand, implement, and analyze knowledge, factual, conceptual, procedural, and metacognitive by curiosity about science, technology, art, culture, and humanities with the insight of humanity, national, state, and civilization-related causes of phenomena and events, as well as applying procedural knowledge in the specific field of study according to their talents and interests to solve problems **(Intellectual Quotient/Knowledge).**
4. Processing, reasoning, and presents it in the realm of the concrete and the abstract associated with the development of the learned in school independently, to act effectively and creatively, and are able to use the method according to the rules of science **(Psychomotor).**

B. Basic Competences and Objectives of Learning

3.1. Basic Competences to Achieve

1.3. To implement the ways to save water sources as per Islamic Principles. **(Spiritual)**

2.3. To show discipline in using water. **(Emotional)**

3.3. To understand the ways to save water sources as per Islamic Principles **(Intellectual)**

4.3. To act the ways to save water sources. **(Psychomotor)**

3.2. The objectives of Teaching are

After observing, explore, negotiate, and communicate, the students are able to:

1.2.1. To determine the Islamic Principles related to the ways of saving water.

1.2.2. To describe the interpretation of Islamic Principles related to the ways of saving water.

1.2.3. To implement the ways to save water sources as per Islamic Principles.

C. Learning Materials

The Qur'an said that we have to eat and to drink water in a proper way not by excess. However, Allah really Hates muslims who do wudu and use water excessively. Nevertheless Islam obliged muslim ummah to do salah and wudu before salah encouraged by using water but Islam also required muslim to use water in a proper way during wudu. Allah had mentioned it at suria Al-'Araf (7) verse 31. The above verse explained clearly in Hadith narrated by Ahmad ibn Hanbal as follows:

> "...Prophet Muhammad PBUH went on trip with Sa'ad ibn Waqqas. When Sa'ad took ritual ablution, Prophet said: don't use the water in excessive manner! Then Sa'ad asked: is there an excessive manner in ritual ablution?, Prophet said: yes, although you done it in river stream".

In the Shariah, there is a responsibility placed on upstream farms to be considerate of downstream users. A farm beside a stream is forbidden to monopolize its water. After withholding a reasonable amount of water for his crops, the farmer must release the rest to those downstream. Furthermore, if the water is insufficient for all of the farms along the stream, the needs of the older farms are to be satisfied before the newer farm is permitted to irrigate.

Both argumentations above are strongly reminding people to not use water in excessive manner. It is one of our behaviour toward water. Other Hadith narrated by Abu Daud also explained about behaviour upon water as follows:

> "...avoid three curses deed i.e. loosen bowels in wellspring, streets, and arbour trees".

Prophet Muhammad PBUH also said, which is narrated by Al-Bukhari:

> "None of you take urine in not flow water and then you take bath in it".

Nowadays, the pollution is not only limited in urinate, loosen bowels, washing dress, and bathing, but also industrial waste contamination, chemical disposal for fertilizer and household needs, crude oil spilled, and etc. But Islam strictly prohibited throws away those pollutions in wellspring, streets (including sea and river), arbour trees, and non-flow water (including water reservoir and pool).

D. Learning Method

1. Learning Approach: Discovery Learning
2. Learning Method/Strategy: Snow ball strategy by listening music, Hypnoteaching strategy, Group Quiz Strategy, Group discussion, Mapping Method.

E. Learning Activities

Activities	*Details of Activities*	*Timing*
Introduction	a. Teacher offering salam b. Asking student to pray together leaded by chief c. Asking student present d. Investigating students preparation to learn e. Questions regarding previous materials **(snow ball strategy by listening music)** f. Delivering the objectives of learning and competence to be achieved and its benefit in daily life. g. Delivering brief materials to learn and its benefits in daily life. h. Delivering scope and assessment technic will be used.	10 mnt
Core Learning	**Contemplation** a. Giving the brainstorming regarding wonderful system of rainfall as proof of Allah existence. **(Hypnoteaching strategy by slow music)** **Observation** a. Students observe pictures provided b. Asking students' opinion regarding pictures **Asking** a. Student requested to ask and make question related to topic. **(Mapping Method)**	30 mnt

	Collecting Information a. Students asked to read the material in their own book. b. Students asked to review dictionary or google translate using mobile and vocabularies table to find meaning of unknown vocabularies. **Reasoning** a. Students requested to share information they get to their group. **(Group Discussion Strategy)** b. Prepare to present the results of these discussions in class. Each group should discuss about: -Way to save water as per Islamic principles. c. Teacher offering some quiz to increase students' comprehension upon material **(Group Quiz Strategy)** **Communicating** a. Students of each group requested to present the result of discussion. b. Students asked to answer questions in exercise page.	
Closing	a. Student asked to summarize the materials on their opinion b. Reflection to learning process attended c. Feedback of learning d. Offering assignment to observe the behaviour of people surround school and home which showing good behaviour toward water, and to write down the commentary on table. e. Delivering the post test rule. f. Du'a leaded by chief of class and closing	5 mnt

F. Tools and Learning Sources

1. *Material Book:* Environmental Education As Per-Islamic Principles; Environmental Education Course For Students of Secondary Madrasa Class X (Brenny Novriansyah: author)
2. Human behaviour in using water observation tools.

G. Assessment

1. Attitude

a. Assessment strategy : Observation
b. Assessment type : Observation
c. Assessment instrument : Observation form

Attitude Assessment Form

No.	*Name of Students*	*1*	*2*	*3*	*4*	*Sum*	*Description*
1							
2							
3							

(1) Honest, score 10–25
(2) Participative, score 10–25
(3) Responsibility, score 10–25
(4) Team work, score 10 – 25

Description: (40–50 = D, 51–60 = C, 61–70 = B, 71–100 = A)

2. Knowledge

Assessment Type: Group Discussion and Essay Questions

a. Group Discussion

Find out the ways to save water as per Islamic principles, determining human behaviour in saving water and knowing how to implement the ways in school environment.

b. Exercise

A. Kindly describe your Answer

1. Why Muslim prohibited using water in excessive manner? (Score: 0 – 20)
2. What are the *dalil*/reasons that Islam prohibited using water excessively? (Score: 0 – 20)
3. Explain about Islam Prohibition regarding contaminating water? (Score: 0 – 20)
4. Describe how should be Muslim behaviour through water! (Score: 0 – 20)
5. How to keep the wealthiest material of water and preserve it? (Score: 0 – 20)

2. Practice

Assessment type: Observation

Observe the proper behaviour and the worst behaviour through water using in your school and environment. Fill the form below:

No.	*Proper Behaviour toward water*	*Worst behaviour toward water*
1		
2		

(Score: 0 – 100)

Attested by, Teacher,
The Principal
(Name) **(Name)**

The characteristic of Good Lesson Planning in Teaching of Islam

Good lesson planning in teaching of Islam have several characteristics as the following:

1. It should be written on special book or typed in one binding book not to be kept in head. Whether you are senior teacher or junior teacher, you will have to write lesson plan in language that used as a medium of teaching.

2. Clearly mention the aims and objectives of learning.
3. It should linked with the previous knowledge and materials.
4. States clearly various steps and techniques of teaching of Islam that the teacher is going to take including evaluation would be provided.
5. Mentioning proper tools and teaching aids that empower teaching of Islam materials and attract student's attention.
6. It should contain suitable organized subject matter.
7. It should be divided into units.
8. It should be provided for activity, students must be given enough scope to be active especially in practicing prayer, reciting Qur'an and Hadith and not make them as passive listeners.
9. The lesson plan should be covered varied abilities levels of students.
10. The plan should indicate the duration of the period, age, subjects and the class.
11. It should be flexible, it is wrong to follow slavishly to plan. The teacher can change his teaching methods if it is needed.
12. The summary of materials should be included by the help of students at the end of teaching process.
13. Includes assignment for students whether in groups or personal.
14. Provided self-evaluation and self-criticism. The teacher should put some questions to himself and find out the answer.
15. lesson plan should be child-centred approach.
16. The teacher should prepare the lesson plan in such a way that various methods and techniques of teaching are incorporated in it.
17. If possible, a lesson-plan should be studded with humorous anecdotes so that there is no boredom during the delivery of the lesson, especially in subjects of *Aqeeda*, *Akhlaq*, *History of Islam, Qur'an & Hadith Tafsir* as those subjects are focused on norms and concept.

Summary

Lesson planning was a foundation of teaching practice in classroom from the beginning day to the last day of learning. Teacher should carefully arrange the best plan for future generation that will be memorable in their student's mind. Indubitably we don't want to cultivate seeds through wrong way and disputable methods that caused crop failure.

Proper lesson plan will help teacher to keep the learning process on track, safely from unwanted waste talking that rob the learning period with useless matters, also ensure the teacher not to dry up and forget a vital point of materials.

REFERENCES

Aggarwal, J.C. 2001. *Principles, Methods and Techniques of Teaching.* New Delhi: Vikas Publishing House Pvt. Ltd., pp. 322–346

Banga, Chaman Lal. 2012. *Teaching of Mathematics.* New Delhi: Shipra Publications, pp. 171-175.

Collins English Dictionary. 1979. Patrick Hanks (ed.) Glasgow: HarperCollins.

Kochar, S.K. 1984. *Teaching of History.* New Delhi: Sterling Publisher Pvt. Ltd., pp. 339-344.

Maunah, Binti (2009). *Metodologi Pengajaran Agama Islam; Metode Penyusunandan Desain Pembelajaran.* Yogyakarta; Teras, p. 3.

Naqvi, Talmeez Fatma. 2010. *Teachers in Classroom: The Perceptual Roadblocks.* New Delhi: Shipra Publications, pp. 100-101.

Sharma, Ram Pratap. 2013. *Methods of Teaching and Evaluation in Social Studies.* New Delhi: Kanishka Publishers, pp. 93-99.

Wikipedia. 2018. Lesson Plan. Retrieved on date: 16.10.2018 from: https://en.wikipedia.org/wiki/Lesson_plan#cite_note-ITC-1

Index